The Great Eagle Calling

Millie Camille Eehn - Toms

Kingdom Enterprises International
www.KingdomEnterprisesInternational.com
Arlington, Texas

The Great Eagle Calling

Copyright © 2009 Millie Toms

Printed in the United States of America.

For information contact Publisher:
Kingdom Enterprises International Publishing
P.O. Box 122181
Arlington, Texas 76012
www.KingdomEnterprisesInternational.com

ISBN 13 Number **978-0-9741274-8-4**

Cover design and graphics, and inside layout design are by the Publisher www.KingdomEnterprisesInternational.com. The photographs featured on the cover, and used throughout the book, were taken by the Author's husband Will Toms. Additional Photo Credits: Page 204 by Danielle Romeyn, Page 8 & 215 by Author Millie Toms.

First Printing 2009

This book is dedicated to the glory of God.
He is more beautiful than I could ever say!

To my husband,
Will Toms of thirty years of our marriage together
&
To our grown children:
Clover Esther & Tim David Jacobs
Naphtali Rebeckah Toms
John William Toms

Also
Dr. John H. & Margaret H. Eehn
Daniel & Kathryn, Westin, Bethany Eehn
David Oliver Eehn
Audrey Lois Toms

And to all my wonderful friends &
Dedicated YWAM Tribalwinds staff
Who made this journey possible!

And to all my beautiful Hopi friends
You know who you are

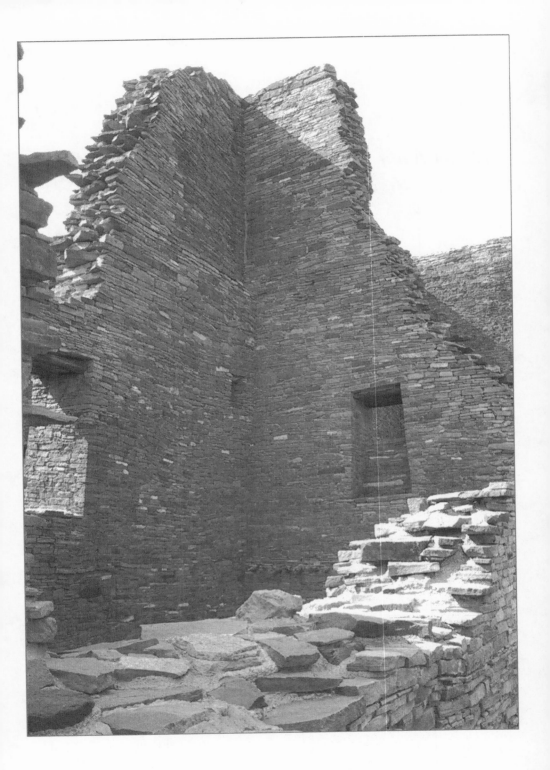

The Great Eagle Calling

Table of Contents

Preface

The Great Eagle Calling

Table of Contents – Continued

Preface

Amongst the Native American nations, there is a belief that the eagles take the prayers of their people. But, amongst the Hopis in the Southwest, they have a story that when the eagle has gone as far as he can, there comes the biggest, the greatest Father Eagle of all called, "Qua-toko". He, then, takes the prayers of the people the rest of the way to the Creator.

We, the human race, once killed the Great Eagle. The Hopis, the oldest tribe in North America, sacrifice eagles every year during their ceremonial dances. This story is to declare God's faithfulness and His unending love towards the Hopi nation, but more than that, to all and every nation on this earth. It is my desire to bring awareness of the Native Americans and their situation, starting with the Hopi. The Native Americans, and the Tribal people groups around the world, need to be part of our God's plan. We believe that they have a key role to play!

I have a desire to tell this story in hope that much interest would be raised concerning our Native American friends whose own story is hardly ever told from a positive point of view. I do not believe that Jesus is white, nor do I believe that anyone should abandon their own culture to become a follower of Him. I do believe that one should cut out the areas of one's culture which grieve our Creator. Most evangelical Christians and other people think the mission field is overseas or across the border. After 400 years of stumbling North

American mission history, we believe that the mission field is also right here in the United States!

There is a huge need to still ask God for the harvesters to come and reach the Native Americans right here, in ways that show honor and respect for these tribal host peoples. It is my hope and desperate prayer that many intercessors would be raised up for the Native Americans. I pray that a flame of fire would be set in place in the hearts of everyone who reads this story -- to intercede, to pray for the original people of this land. Very importantly, we need to stop patronizing Native believers, as though they have nothing to offer, and start partnering with them to reach the World.

There is a nobility and wisdom that the Lord has given to believing Native Americans which is about to explode and be used for God's kingdom purposes. Even in Europe, Israel, Pakistan and China where Christians are not welcome, they have opened their arms wide to have Native American followers of Christ come to their nations. In Israel, our Native American Christian friends were able to even go into the Knesset (parliament) with their 120 drums when, at the very same time, missionaries were being kicked out of Israel. In China, at the International Arts Festival, thousands of Chinese pressed in to be able to see the Native American followers of Christ with their feathers, beads and regalia, dancing their prayers to Jesus. Europe boasts of having Native American clubs and the Germans imitate Indian bead work with an amazing degree of precision. It is as though much of the world is waiting for their unique culture, songs and dance to come to their land with the message of Christ, the living God.

We at YWAM TRIBAL WINDS are praying for our Native American brothers and sisters in Christ to rise up and take their place. We want them to know that they are priests unto the Creator and redeemed by the blood of the Lamb. We believe that the Europeans and the others have had their chance to be God's known evangelists. Now, we believe it is the time for the Native Americans to take their *inheritance and go to the nations and make Jesus' name known! After all, Jesus was a tribal man and paid the price for everyone on earth to give us life, full and meaningful! Jesus is the Great Eagle, who was sacrificed once and for all!*

We are in need of those who want to learn about God's heart for these overlooked host peoples. We need those who are willing to put aside the white man's ways of doing things; those who are willing to recognize that the Creator has also given the Native people inherently beautiful ways in which they can worship Christ. We want those who are willing to say, "Perhaps, we will not only hear Handel's Messiah in heaven, but all the Native American instruments and music; the high pitch Powwow songs and the low, gentle chants of the Pueblos, in heaven also."

Even though there have been hundreds of years of evangelism to the tribes, approximately 2-5% of the Native Americans are believers. This is outrageous! God's Word should be much more effective than this! The love of God surely should affect more hearts than this. How have we, as a nation and as Christians, brought God's message in the wrong way? How have we misrepresented God? We all need to come together and earnestly pray and seek God regarding this matter, so that true reconciliation movements can happen amongst the first nations peoples and the Christians, of North America. I believe the Lord is on the move like Aslan, the Lion in C.S. Lewis' Narnia books.

I will also mention that it may be politically correct to use the words, "Native Americans" or the "First Nations" in Canada or the "Indigenous people" rather than the word, "Indians". However, when we have asked many of our friends concerning how they would like to be addressed, although, some prefer the name, "the Native Americans" in the U.S., many say that they do not mind either way, and call themselves, Indians. So, I will interchangeably use all these words.

Also, the word, "Christian" is often an unwelcome word amongst our Native American friends; as this word carries much baggage with so much bad history of broken trust and atrocities in the name of Christ. However, for lack of a better word, I will go ahead and use this word. I will often substitute this with, a "Follower of Jesus" or a "Believer in Christ," as those phrases more simply describe who we and they are, without the baggage.

God is doing amazing things amongst the Native peoples of North America and the indigenous peoples of the world. We are thrilled to be a part of this exciting adventure! We are seeing that unreached tribal people groups around the world have the world view very similar to the Native Americans.

We do understand that God also loves all the nations, and that He calls different ones to have the same kind of passion for various nations, as we have with the Hopi and the Native American nations. However, for those who do not have a clear mandate, we ask that you pray about coming and being right here in North America; not so much to proselytize, but to simply be their friends, to pray for their people and to point them to Jesus. It may be wise, and perhaps, even more effective to reach the Native Americans first, and let them take their stories of the Creator, Father and His Son to the ends of the earth!

It was never my intention to write a book when we first arrived on the Hopi reservation. The call to write this book, however, was as strong as the call to come to Hopiland. At times, this book may not sound very encouraging, and may even seem depressing. However, I have desired to be honest about all that I have gone through, both in joy and in my despair which I have felt in my being, rather than pretending to be whom I am not. I wanted to keep the integrity of all that God has been teaching me, even if that meant possibly being judged, because of some of the difficult issues and controversial matters.

This book will hopefully challenge you on many levels, as I have been challenged.

It is hard for the believers, in Hopi, to survive or thrive as they are persecuted by the traditional Hopis for turning to Jesus, and by the Church who insists that they must look white, throwing away all the Hopi ways. And yet, I am most confident that a beautiful season has already arrived when a Hopi can be a true Hopi, meaning, "The People of Peace."

In my efforts to live and work amongst the Hopi and indigenous people, I had to wrestle with God on many levels. I often come away limping like Jacob after he had wrestled with the Lord; we should limp a little when we wrestle with the Word of God. The Lord has been so good and kind to us. O Praise Him!

*My heart is overflowing with a good theme
I recite my composition concerning the King
My tongue is the pen of a ready writer.
(Psalm 45: 1)*

Chapter 1

The Creator of the Universe Calling

We are going to an ancient place where the eagles are sacrificed. This is our moving day, and we had just turned east off of Leupp Road at a small highway sign, towards Kykotsmovi village. Our Father, the Creator of the universe is calling me and my family to this ancient land, and now, we were driving to this place in the Northern Arizona high desert, to a house which I had never seen before in my life. We must drive almost one hundred miles northeast From Flagstaff to get to the Hopi Indian reservation. There is only one gas station in a small Navajo town called Leupp about 45 miles from the town of Flagstaff.

We have to pass through this land of the "Din'e", or Navajo people, in order to get into the Hopi reservation. The Din'e people are the newest comers to this land, arriving around four to five hundred years ago. They were a nomadic people who built their shelters and moved their camps often with their flocks for grazing, who finally surrounded the Hopi nation. Later, the majority of the land was given to the Din'e by our U.S. government where their encampments were established. Hopis and Navajos, the first and the last book-ends of all the nations are right next door to each other.

I looked in my rear view mirror to take a glance at our three children who had all fallen asleep in the back seat. And then, suddenly, I couldn't stop crying for the next 47 miles of high desert land which seemed so barren to my soul; I heard that there was a Japanese Internment Camp near this area during World War II.

I was crying not because I was unsure as to why we have come for I knew without a doubt that we had a calling to come to this land. Even still, I had no idea how our children would fare in this land. Would they be loved? Would they be accepted by the Hopi kids? Would they be happy here in this high desert land away from so many things they took for granted like the ocean? We drove on and then turned into the road which has been since then, marked with a mile marker "47". Then, I saw the house which was to be our home; I had never seen this house before. Only Will had seen it and reported to me that it was such a perfect house for us and I trusted him.

It had always been my heart's desire to own a place of our own. We had a very small but a lovely place in Santa Barbara. If it had not been for the persistent suggestions of our friend, David Mitchell, who kept insisting that we look into a "County Moderate Income Housing Project," we would have never purchased our condo. It was truly a miracle! I loved our cozy home, filled with antiques and pictures.

I thank the Lord that He allowed me to have my heart's desire for awhile for it is always easier for me to give it up, once I had it, for I no longer felt deprived. If anyone had asked me whether I wanted to live on the Hopi Reservation, I would have said they were crazy. And yet, as I prayed for the Hopi nation, I found myself longing to be on the reservation with such deep love for the people that I knew this had to be from the Lord. I thank Marcy O'Hara and

Gail Callaway who faithfully prayed with me weekly for the Hopis back in Santa Barbara.

Will and I had just come back from a week-long trip out to Hopiland for a Spring break. The small Mennonite Church in the village of Bacavi had been possibly offered to us by the lady pastor who was leaving there soon; she had told us that she could not stay in Hopiland, another winter season. The church and the parsonage were all that I had hoped for and so much more. I had prayed that God will let us have that country home, but instead, we were moving into the house in the village of Kykostmovi which was called the "Schirmer House". Everyone knew Daniel Schirmer who was the first ordained Hopi pastor and his wife Amy who had died, leaving the house vacant for almost fifteen years before we finally moved in.

The Ancient People

I had once heard that the ancient people of the Southwest had disappeared all together like the dinosaurs. The "Anasazi" people (in Navajo meaning, "the Ancient enemy") have not disappeared as

some may have believed. These cliff dwellers, who left so many beautiful, thousand year old, rock houses and spectacular cliff castles in the four corners area of Arizona, Colorado, Utah and New Mexico, are still very much alive and well. They are the remaining twenty small Pueblo tribes including the Hopi. The archeologists have found artifacts and pottery shards amongst the

Anasazi ruins which trace these ones back to the people group called the Hopi in Northern Arizona.

This is the land where the eagles are sacrificed yearly to this very day. Our US government recognizes the Hopi as the ancient people group who ceremonially sacrificed eagles before Columbus ever landed in this hemisphere. Therefore, the Hopis are the only people in the United States allowed to kill eagles every year. Unlike some other tribes who had been moved to Oklahoma through their 'Trail of Tears", the Hopis have never been relocated by the US government.

They chose this high desert plateau with inhospitable winds and sand everywhere. All you can see is the color brown. It is the land of many ceremonial dances: Buffalo, Deer, Snake, Kachina and Flute, and many others.

We had to first get up to the town of Flagstaff which is 7,000 feet above sea level. This is where the Hopis also once lived as what is left of their cliff rock houses are displayed at Walnut Canyon National Park off of Interstate 40. One would never think that such a mountainous town with its snow capped San Francisco peaks, which are sacred to the Native peoples of this region, exists in Arizona. Most everyone, as I also have always thought, thinks that Arizona is all desert, like the city of Phoenix.

In fact, Flagstaff has the largest Ponderosa Pine forest in the world and also a huge area of Aspen groves which turns into magnificent fall colors in its due season. It also has the famous Lowell Observatory which found the planet Pluto. Flagstaff is the gateway to the Grand Canyon,

The fall colors are spectacular in the meadows up in Flagstaff mountains

a stones throw away from the red rocks of Sedona, and the Painted Desert is a bit to the north. It still has the charm of a small town with an old railroad station still in use. The historic, winding Route 66 goes right through the whole town.

America, streets paved with gold?

My original home, as a child, was in S. Korea. My father came to study Music at the University of Oregon and later at the University of Southern California, leaving my mother and my two younger brothers and me behind in Seoul. I think he would have loved having his own orchestra as I used to see him fiercely conducting an invisible symphony in our living room, with his eyes closed and with his head-set over his ears. Then, one day, we all came to America with the help of a kind lady, Esther Kim whom we called Aunty Esther, in 1968.

I was happy to be here in this country even though the apartment in Los Angeles was nothing like the mansion I had imagined in my mind. My father had sent me a picture once from America; he was standing on the green lawn, in front of a great looking building. Only the very wealthy in Korea could live in a house with grass yards. I had thought that whole apartment complex in the picture was our own mansion with the stairways leading up to my own room with beautiful porcelain dolls. I could hardly believe the rude awakening when I had to share a bedroom with my two brothers with nothing but bare floor, bare walls and two single beds on the first night when we arrived.

I was, however, very impressed that my dad picked us up in his forest green color Oldsmobile which looked like a Cadillac to me. I remember another Korean friend told me once that when he first arrived at the Los Angeles Airport as a child and was driven through the night, that he thought the round lane dividers discs on the freeways were real gold. So, he said to himself, "Wow, the people were really telling the truth when they said that America is very rich."

Santa Barbara is where we have lived for seventeen years before going to Hopi. It is one of only few places in the U.S.A. where the mountains meet the ocean. The average temperature is 72 F. all year around.
It could not have been more perfect for Will who loves to do rock-climbing and all the ocean activities.

Right of Passage

In the spring of 1994, my husband, Will, had called me at my work in Santa Barbara. I was surprised to hear from him because he had gone up to the snowy Sierra Nevada Mountains to do the yearly wilderness staff training, within our Sea & Summit Expeditions ministry and he should have been where there was no phone service. I know this as this is how Will and I met doing these Expeditions and Rock climbing with the probation kids and other youth at-risk kids up in the High Sierras.

That day, he called me in a hoarse voice saying that he needed to come home and tell the kids and me something NEW that God was doing. I was curious as to what he had gotten himself into.

Our lives with Jesus have been an Odyssey
Will's sailing trip with Sea & Summit Expeditions brought youth at risk out to the Channel Islands off of Santa Barbara (1977). What seems to be the seagull is really an image of a crack in a big rock where S&S did rock climbing with those same at risk young adults. Will double exposed to produce this photo.

This is where a Native American girl was found. She was living alone for eighteen years with a wild dog and a black raven on San Nicholas Island. Her whole family and the tribe had been slaughtered. She was the last of her tribe. She was taken to the Santa Barbara Missios and there is a book called, The Island of the Blue Dolphins which is about her life.

Will with our children, John and Naphtali, in the Southwest many years before we had a call to Arizona

for he is a man who will step out and do whatever he feels the Lord is telling him to do

When I came home and saw what he looked like, I became suspicious and put my seat out on the fringe of our living room in order to examine him as he spoke. Will shared with me and our three children of 9, 11, and 13 years, something we had never heard before. He shared how God had awakened him in the middle of the night, first with two dreams, while up on a snowy peak. Then later in the Sierra foothills above the town of Bishop the Lord challenged him to not "fear men" but to "only fear God." God took him through what he could only describe as a "right of passage" or an initiation into things of God which were unique to Native Americans. I was glad when I heard that he made himself accountable by waking up the other staff to keep an eye on him and to pray for him.

Don't fear men, fear God

This was up in the high desert like terrain of the Sierra foothills and there were many sharp desert plants all around. Will said that the Lord, who identified Himself as YAHWEH (Exodus 3:14), had him run a number of times "in the Spirit". I knew that Will could run fast because his teammates from the Navy Seal team told me that Will always came in first during their training runs. I asked the Lord in my heart whether He was a sadistic God who would hurt his children, because Will's legs were all cut up and even had a big gouge in one shin. I was surprised to get such a quick response from the Lord with the reply saying, "Look at Jacob, I made a mark on him; he limped for the rest of his life."

When we were in ministry back in Santa Barbara many years ago, we all went to see an Australian movie called, "Gallipoli." The Victoria Theatre was packed out that night and it was standing room only even on the balcony. It was such a tragic ending that all the audience sat frozen in silence. Then, all of a sudden, I saw Will get up out of his seat and run up to the front and get up on the stage. He began to shout to the audience and said that we were all like these young runners who were getting killed. But, there was an answer and that his name is Jesus. As soon as the name of Jesus was mentioned, the guard or the Manager of the theater came down the aisle telling Will to please get off the stage. The audience began getting up and leaving in droves. Will shouted out to the audience that he will be outside if anyone wanted to speak to him. I wanted to sink and hide in my seat. Only a couple of people came, a gentle lady who was disappointed that there was no room for public speaking and another middle eastern man who wanted to argue that Jesus was not the way.

We later discussed what happened. I felt that action was done out of an un-restrained zeal and it did not produce anything that was profitable for the kingdom of God (who can say but God?) that we can see. Besides, I did not particularly like being embarrassed unnecessarily. And yet, I could not help but to respect this man who had dared to do what he felt the Holy Spirit was telling him to do; I would bet that not one out of a thousand men would have had the courage to do what Will did that evening.

Yahweh "Hayah"

So, I was not all together surprised when this desert experience happened. He was told to proclaim YAH in the four directions, and led by the Spirit, he was dancing and chanting HAYAH, HAYAH, HAYAH. The number "Four" is very important to the Native Americans, but Will did not know that, then. Will said at that point, he had to stop everything and test the spirit thinking, "I've had my drug days. I don't want to go there again." But, he soon knew this was the same Spirit he had loved and served ever since he came to know Jesus in his heart. And he said that the Lord spoke in his heart.

When Moses ran into the burning bush in Exodus 3:14, God said to Moses, "I am YAWEH", meaning I Am who I Am or possibly I Am Becoming. And the root word for YAHWEH (which the Spirit pronounced to Will as "Ya Way") is HAYAH ("Hay Ya"). We did not know it then, but the Lord had Will cry out in the Four Directions what all the Native Americans chant in their songs saying, "Hayah, Hayah, Hayah." One would hear these words, and variations on them, repeated again and again at all the Powwows, and also in all the Pueblo/American Indian songs.

We believe that when the Lord dispersed the nations at Babel and blessed them with their various languages that the Native Americans, inherently have been given the name of the Creator to call out in their songs and they have been singing these words back to Him for thousands of years. The Word of God says that "He is the Alpha and Omega, the beginning and the end". I think it is uncanny that if one should read, "HAYAH" backwards, it still will be exactly the same! When I am singing HAYAH with my Native friends, I am saying, "Hallelujah" to our Lord.

Variously known as a Hopi Warrior shield, Peace symbol or Peoples of the world: white, black, yellow and red

Lord, did I marry a crazy man?

When Will had told us that YAH that night was appearing like his Indian Chief Father, I thought he had gone nuts. So I did not hesitate to again ask God in my heart, "I just wanted a godly man, did I marry a crazy man?" And again, I was given a very swift reply which was "No, he is not crazy. Trust him." Will talked about a number of experiences such as where he danced, circling in the spirit to the right, and then circling to the left, saying words like "a warrior is brave and strong" and "a squaw is gentle and kind".

He proceeded to tell us that night that all he wanted to do was to simply obey the Lord with absolutely everything he had in him. So he ran, danced and proclaimed His Name, YAH, until he nearly lost his voice. I asked again, "Father, are you sure I did not marry a crazy man?" This third time, God ran out of patience with me, and I felt a quiet but very strong rebuke as though someone had hit my stomach, and I heard Him in my heart.

"Don't be like Michal, let him dance!"

The words were, "Millie, don't be like Michal! Let him dance!" Michal was Saul's daughter and King David's wife. She was ashamed of David when he danced with all his might, almost naked, through the streets when the Ark of the Covenant was coming back into Israel. (2 Samuel 6:14) God did not want me to be embarrassed about what was happening. I did not want to be like Michal who despised her husband, David, for dancing with all his might. No, I didn't want to be like Michal who never had children to the day of her death. After all, our God is a wild God! Look at John the Baptist and Elijah; they are not church pew sitting gentle and quiet guys. God was doing a paradigm shift in our world as He pleased, and either we were going to follow Him or quench His Spirit and walk away.

Dreams and visions for the next two years

After that day, Will and some others around us began to have a series of dreams about the First Nations' people for over two years. These were dreams that a white man could not make up on his own volition. In one dream, an Indian man in the Amazon walking towards a hut with a cross on it, fixed his eyes ahead and said, "I need my black spine cleaned." Each time after a dream, we would ask, "Lord, do you want us to go to the Amazon, the Philippines etc.?" But, we sensed that we were still in a waiting period to simply watch what He was unfolding, still yet to come with more.

We even found out about the Ainu people, the indigenous people of Japan because of the last dreams Will had which were

12

taking us roughly around the Pacific Rim. I am of Korean descent and, having been born not far from Japan, had no idea that there were "Indians" who have Bear clans just like the Hopis and many other Native American nations, in Hokkaido, Japan. These are the things which the Lord Himself can reveal for His purposes to be done which we know not of. All I know is that is this was about "love"; His love which He wanted so desperately to reveal on this earth.

"It's the Hopis and watch out for religious spirits"

It was at the end of the first year of dreams and visions that Will heard the Lord speak to him one night. "You are going to the Hopis; there are other tribes and watch out for religious spirits." (As it turned out, we found out that the religious spirits were not just in the Hopi ways, but also in some of the denominational churches.) I personally did not know who the Hopis were, so it was amazing to find that they were Native Americans located in this windy desert land of Northern Arizona. They had been led to this land thousands of years ago, and have the oldest continually dwelt settlements in all of North America.

So, it is simply a lack of knowledge when outsiders come and ask for forgiveness on behalf of their white government, who made the Hopi move to this inhospitable land. There is no history of "the trail of tears" with the Hopi as with the Navajo and some of the other tribes. The Hopis chose this land for themselves over one thousand years ago on top of these mesas in the middle of the high Arizona desert.

The Hopi also still continue much of their calendar year cycle of dances, ceremonies and initiations as they did thousands of years ago. All the children are given opportunity to be initiated in the kivas (underground ceremonial chambers with a ladder coming up). The men and women belong to different societies. And I did not know that many of the cliff dwelling ruins in the Southwest were built by the "Anasazi," who are the ancestors of the Hopi, or "Hisatsinom" in Hopi. Many houses are on top of the three main mesas, similar to the Tibetan houses, and they are made of stones quarried from the desert sandstone.

Our Children hear God for themselves

We did not want to drag our children out to the Hopi reservation, as the last thing we would want is to have rebellious children out there when we're trying to do the Lord's work. Ever since they were very little, every morning, we used to spend ten or twenty minutes of devotion time with our kids before they went off to school in Santa Barbara. I would see the kids clapping their hands and singing, with their legs sticking out on our couch, as their little feet were not able to touch the floor yet as they were still small. After a couple or a few songs, they would read the Word together out loud and Will would pray and bless them, and off to school they went! I imagine that these few moments every morning, added up to many hours in their life time of drawing close to our God.

They were by now, in 1996, eleven, thirteen and fifteen years old. It was during this time that Will and I asked the children, at our morning devotion, to ask in prayer, "God, I Know that you called my parents to go to Hopiland, but am I supposed to go?" We were certain that our kids would hear God's voice for themselves. After two weeks when we all got together in the morning and asked them, "So, what did the Lord tell you?" both John and Clover said to us, "Yes, God is telling me that I am supposed to go." When it came to Naphtali, she sighed a deep sigh and said, "I don't want to go, but He is telling me that I am supposed to go."

The Jewels holding me back

There was one more thing which was holding me back from coming to Hopi. I had a goal of finishing my degree and I felt that I should eventually also get my Masters and PhD, in Counseling or

Education. One evening at our "Teddy Bears" (Bearing One another's Burdens) Ladies Fellowship in Santa Barbara, Susan Kuroda who had been hosting us for almost two years in her home, invited our two Pastors, Dan Hodgeson and Marty Reitzin to pray over the twelve ladies who had been meeting.

Dan and Marty are two amazing pastors who have loved so many people in our community for over thirty five years and served so faithfully without much recognition. I do not know whether I have felt so loved and accepted unconditionally by any pastors as I have with Dan and Marty. When we had invited Dan over to our condominium soon after Will's "right of passage" experience, so that he could hear the story and let us know what he thought, all Dan said was "Yes, this is of the Lord. This is not out of line with what the Old Testament prophets experienced. " The Lord spoke through Marty ("Bro Jew") that evening to me. Marty saw a picture of me grasping and reaching for some jewels. Marty said that Jesus was saying, "Millie, turn around. Open your mouth and serve me," while Jesus was standing behind me. My heart was grieved beyond measure that I was going after other jewels while my back was turned towards Jesus.

Later that evening, the Lord spoke in my heart and said, "Those jewels are not for you - diamonds, rubies and sapphires." He showed me that those jewels represented my "Education" which I thought would bring me financial security, honor and status. This message came on the eleventh hour for I had an appointment the very next day at 9:00 AM to meet with a Curriculum Counselor at a College in that City.

God was merciful to me and to our marriage. If He had not shown this to me, I would have resisted in following Will to Hopiland. I may have tried to convince Will that I need to first finish my Education because after all, it would benefit God's work that I would be able to serve the Lord better. It is only God who knows the hearts of His children. He knew the weakness in my heart which had

15

desired wealth, honor from human beings and status in the community. He was merciful! Now, I am free to live for God.

Our new home in Hopiland

We moved into Hopiland in August of 1996. "Hopi" is an all inclusive word which includes the land, the people and all the cultural ceremonies and dances and all other aspects of their clans and family lives. Therefore, one does not need to say "Hopiland or Hopi Indian reservation or Hopi people or Hopi religion. The word, "Hopi" would include all these essential matters. However, when in Rome, I should do as the Romans. For the sake of those in the outside world, I will go ahead and use the other words to clarify whether I am talking about the land or the people.

Four other men from our church had come with Will to fix the plumbing, a few weeks prior to us moving into the Schirmer house. Afterwards, our transmission went out on our car so Will was stuck back in Flagstaff while the other four men came back to Santa

Barbara. Before Will got home, I heard from all four men who told me separately that we could not possibly move into that Schirmer house because it was too moldy with water damage and piles of mice dung and dust and that it would make our children sick. When I heard this for the fourth time, I went home and sat and cried quietly on our stairway in our Santa Barbara townhouse, after the children had gone to bed that evening.

Will called that same night and said, "Honey, we have the most perfect house in Hopiland and you would love it. I think you're going to do beautiful things with it. God has given us truly one of the best houses out here!" Indeed there were molds and mice dung when we arrived. But I felt that Will was like Caleb in the Bible who said, "We should by all means go up and take possession of the land, for we shall surely overcome it". (Numbers 13:17-33) All the other spies said, "There are giants in the land and the people who live there are too strong." Our four friends were certainly not like these ten spies without faith. They also knew that we were to enter the Promised Land, but were simply concerned for us and our children

The day we were moving in, the wind was blowing so hard that day, a small sand dune had piled inside the doorway in our living room. It was no surprise to hear that the sand was right up to the door knob when the men came to fix the plumbing before we moved in and they had to dig the door out. We have had to take out and take apart the door-knobs only to find a handful of sand rushing out when our keys would not work.

Will drove the biggest U-Haul truck we could find so that I could bring all my things, as I thought we may be there for a life time. We came to live and be buried here someday. It was ten years later, however, that we realized that God was not wanting us to be in Hopi to lead the work, but to train the believers to rise up, and then go so that they would be the leaders themselves, rather than perpetually being dependent on the outsiders.

I asked the Lord whether I should sell everything. However, in praying, I believed that He told me three times to go ahead and take all my furniture and tea cups and make ourselves a home in Hopiland. I felt that He said to me, "I told you to go. Just obey and go and be yourself." I had no idea how these familiar things would be of such comfort to all of us later. We had a safe and cozy home while the wind was blowing outside like mad and all we could see was sand everywhere sometimes for many days and weeks. It did not help that we had a hole somewhere in a window which made such an awful howling noise.

It is almost impossible for anyone to come and have a house to live in Hopiland unless one is in a medical or educational field with the Hopi tribe and the housing is included by the Tribe. But, with God, all things are possible!

Daniel Schirmer, the first Hopi ordained pastor

We thank the Lord for Daniel and Amy Schirmer's two daughters and husbands, Ruth & Harlan Bohnee and Elaine Torchbearer & Ed Ryder who opened up the house for us and kept their promise to their father, whose last wish was that this house be only be rented out to only those in God's service. What is strange is that there were others who were in Christian service and had inquired but did not get this house. So, we trust that it was simply God's timing.

According to these two daughters, their father, Daniel Schirmer, after graduating from BIOLA College, was the first Hopi ordained pastor. Daniel was born up at Old Oraibi village, which is the oldest continually dwelt settlement in all of North America. When Daniel was born, his mother died giving him birth. In those days, the Hopi people had believed that the child was demon possessed when this happened and would bury the baby alive with the mother. Daniel's father loved his son and felt pity on him and ran down to Kykotsmovi village below Old Orabi. He found Amy

Schirmer, a German missionary, and asked her to go up and rescue the baby. She did so, adopted the baby, and named him Daniel Schirmer.

Pastor Daniel and Uberta Quimayousi

Pastor Daniel and his wife, Uberta Quimayousi had been ministering in Hopiland for over thirty years in the village of Hotevilla when we arrived. We were able to meet them the first time when we came out to Arizona to do the initial scouting trip after hearing the call that it was the Hopis. We did some research and found out about Jonathan and Molly Eckstrom, the Wycliffe Bible Translators in Tucson, who had translated the Hopi New Testament many years ago. Jonathan told us that there was only one indigenous Hopi pastor who established a church without any help from the white denominations. He also told us that this quiet and reserved Pastor may not give us an audience.

So, a couple of days later, we tested this out and came and looked for Daniel and Uberta in the village of Hotevilla on Thanksgiving Day in 1995. As providence would have it, we found out that they had raised a Korean daughter who spoke better Hopi than many of the Hopis themselves. Apparently, Uberta's younger brother had married a Korean lady during his military service days. Pastor Daniel, as he walked us out after the meal at the church, gently touched the end of my hair and said, "You have black hair just like us, Hopi." I knew that somehow we had started a friendship and that he was even intimate in his own shy way.

We started attending their church with our three children once we moved into the Schirmer House. At first, we did not know whether they'd let us continue to attend their church. Uberta told me that they used to tell the other "Pahanas" (white people or outsiders), after a couple of times of attending, that they should go elsewhere for this was a Hopi church and that they only spoke Hopi. But, they never told us to go elsewhere and they let us stay in order for us to come alongside and serve.

I believe all Hopi Christians have paid a heavy price to follow Christ in this land where their own ceremonies and dances and the community family and clan system is so heavily in place. But, out of all those who paid the price of rejection, I believe that there may be none who paid a heavier price than Daniel and Uberta, to establish church in such a traditional village of Hotevilla on top of the Third Mesa. They simply call it "Hotevilla Gospel Church."

Daniel Quimayousi was Antelope society and one of the snake dancers. This dance is still held to this day. The men go out and capture the snakes including rattlesnakes in the wild and pray, holding these snakes in their hands and in their mouths. Some of the snakes are able to slither around in the village plaza where the people are standing around. This snake dance is no longer held in Hotevilla because Daniel, who would have been the snake priest, rejected this role after he had become a follower of Jesus.

Daniel Quimayousi became a Christian while he was doing construction work in California. Like many of the Hopi Christian men, he had been struggling with alcohol and seeking a way out. When he and Uberta came back to their childhood village of Hotevilla and tried to start a church, they had many trials. Sometimes, the "Mongwi" or Chief would come into their little stone house where they were meeting in this traditional village and tell them that they must go somewhere else. Other times, the village people caught birds and loosed them through the windows so that the birds would fly around and disturb the service. Another time, some people tried to cut the old elm tree down that was next to the house, but the tree would not be cut down because it had a big knot. Another time, people tried pouring gasoline to burn it down, but the tree did not burn. Uberta once told me that God chose Daniel because he was stubborn and God knew he would not quit. I want to be like Daniel and Uberta.

This Christmas in 1996 turned out to be the only Christmas we would spend with Pastor Daniel Quimayousi. However, it was paramount that he called our family up to the front of the church and announced us as the newest members of Hotevilla Gospel Church at the Christmas Eve program in front of the biggest village crowd of the year.

We did not know then, that Pastor Daniel would go home to be with the Lord only one year after we arrived in Hopiland. Uberta called me from the Flagstaff hospital three in the morning and asked me to come and be with her. I remember driving almost 100 miles from Hopi to Flagstaff and I was praying and asking the Lord, not to take Pastor Daniel yet.

It was that same turn off on Highway 2, at Leupp Rd. where I had first cried in coming to Hopiland with our kids asleep in the back that I was crying again hard enough that I almost ran right into the dead-end sign. I loved this man who took us under his wings and called us up in front of the biggest crowd we ever had at our Christmas program at the Church and announced us as the newest family members of their Congregation. I felt it was his and Uberta's way of saying that they love and accept us. What an honor that was! I feel as though the Lord had brought our family to be able to assist Uberta so that she didn't have to carry on the work by herself.

Chapter 2

I Can Hear the Drums and Singing

We had our first Sunday School with the children from the village. Seven children besides our three kids were picked up as I drove around. I am so thankful for this new beginning. Thank you, Lord.

I was concerned that the children would not come back, but almost everyone and a couple more new ones showed up the next week. Naphtali, 13, played the guitar with me and Clover, 15, and Julie had a small class of their own, and Johnny, 11, helped as well. Arnold and Michael did not come to Sunday school today because they went to help their father out in the field to plant corn.

Some months later, I realized that I let bitterness come into my heart for the children who seem to have no concern for other people's things. We have cigarette burnt holes in our trampoline, coins stolen out of our cars, and now, my car door will cost over

$1,000 to get it fixed in Flagstaff for one of the kids had opened it when they were told not to get in my car. This was the best car I ever had. It was only seven years old when we bought it out of a Used Car lot back near Solvang, California.

There is a Dance in Hotevilla again today. Only Alyssa came to Sunday school and two of Sylvia's grandkids. When I was taking Alyssa home, I got stuck in the village with my car stopped with about 120 Katchinas walking right in front of my car to go into the Village Plaza to dance. Alyssa quickly looked down and hid her face with her hand saying that she is not supposed to look at the Katchinas. (Katchinas, Kachinas or Katsinas are Hopi men who dress up to represent spirits of all living things including esteemed ancestors.)

Polacca village is hosting an "Indian Day" this weekend. Isn't everyday an "Indian Day" out here? Anyhow, it was amazing how God had sealed my heart not to be disappointed when not one single child showed up for Sunday school. The number was not where my security laid, but pleasing the Father.

When I went to pick up one of the Sunday school kids, one girl came out of the house and told me that she could no longer come to Church. It is not because she does not want to. It grieved my heart, but the Lord comforted me.

I can hear the drums and the singing now from our home, in the Kykotsmovi village Plaza outside at 9:30 PM. There must be a night Dance. And yet, what a peaceful feeling it is to have God's presence right in our home. The children did beautiful chalk paintings on the basketball court today. It was a nice sunny day to sit and watch the children draw as the wind picked up. I could hardly believe that I was sitting, watching the mesas and the desert in Arizona. Arizona would have been the last place that I would have chosen to live; I had no idea the variety of the beauty in this State. I went for a jog in the village this afternoon. It felt good to walk and see all the houses and the children playing. I feel as though, a stranger, and yet, at home here now all at the same time.

No Electricity by choice in this Village

Tonight, we had a Video night for the children at Church. Russ Toews, the Mennonite pastor at Bacavi, helped me set up the generator so we can be sure to have enough power to run the VCR and the TV. It was a good thing because the light eventually did go off from our solar power, so the generator was needed. Whenever we've had longer Church services or events, we have had to worry about losing power and we often, did. Sometimes, someone would have to rush out to their car and shine their head-lights into the Church building while the others are lighting the kerosene Lanterns. There is electricity at the Community store and at the Elementary School but there is no electricity, paved roads or running water in this Village. Every year, the village people have voted not to have these white men's ways in order to not become dependent on them.

Life's necessities

We all woke up early to drive into Flagstaff to do all our errands. Clover had a Dentist appointment. And then we needed to go to Odegaard's Sewing machine and Vacuum shop, and to a Pet store to get a gold fish for Naphtali and a dog collar for Judith's puppy, Walmart for a lot of odd 'n' ends items, Sam's to do bulk food shopping, Safeway to get food items which Sam's does not have, the Public Library to return books and tapes and to a cheap fast food restaurant to grab a bite to eat and to the bank!

A Nightmare and Dead dog

This morning, when we woke up, Will said he had a bad nightmare. Then, when he went outside, he saw three beer cans lined up in our driveway. It is illegal to have possession of alcohol on this reservation. It was clear that someone was right outside during the night. This is not the first time and yet, the Lord always protects us.

> In Peace, I will both lie down and sleep,
> For You alone, O lord, make me dwell in safety
> (Psalm 4:8)

Somehow, I sensed something dark that day as soon as I woke up in the morning. Will and I went to help the Hopi Mission School Highway Clean up effort. We were assigned an area under the bridge where we found some marked graffiti. I found a dead dog with its head decapitated, in a trash bag which made an awful stench. The Police man who came later to our home was very nice and explained to us that this is not the first time to find dead things and that some people are into some satanic things. That awful stench stayed with me all the rest of the day and I felt nauseated.

The Song - The Battle Belongs to the Lord!

The inmates love to sing the song, "The Battle belongs to the Lord" by Jamie Owens Collins. It is their most favorite song and they request to sing it again and again. One night at the Jail ministry, they sang that song twice with me, and then the third time, as I accompanied them with my guitar; they sang the song all by themselves. And at the end, spontaneously, broke out cheering and clapping.

Another night's ministry at the jail was a total disaster. Or, at least, I thought my song leading time was. I felt sick all of a sudden so that I had to ask our team to come up and pray for me in the middle of a song. It says in Philippians, "Not to be anxious about anything..." I began to give the Lord all my anxious thoughts. He is able to deliver!

The most important thing

My heart is sad because I knew I had forgotten the most important thing yesterday and that the Gospel, the Good news of Jesus could have been so much more effective if I had only sat in His presence awhile and listened. I felt like I was grieving all day that I had made so many other things so important that I had disregarded Him. Oh Lord, forgive and work in spite of me.

There was a sudden gust of strong winds, then, the rain began to envelop our entire village. It was beautiful to sit in front of my red desk and watch the rain fall with the buttes in the back ground. I sang aloud, "I sing a new song to the Lord my God; I lift my voice to Jesus, my King. I bow my face at the footstool of the Lamb; I lay down my life at the altar of God. I worship you, oh, I worship you." It is an amazing thing to have a little pond in front of our house.

Both, Princess Diana and Mother Teresa's funerals were this week- two very different lives. I wonder how they would fare before the throne room of God. Much good works have been done with the poorest of the poor in India by Mother Teresa. However, what we may think as good works may not necessarily mean what we think to the Lord. And perhaps, what we may think are the disdainful lives, God may see differently through His compassion from knowing where they've been and what they're made of.

A Card game and a Cowboy

This morning, Clover and John went to help with the Cow Round-up with Melissa on the horses. The kids have enjoyed their 4-H Horse-riding Club with Melissa who is a teacher at the Hopi Mission School. Ida Walking Bear came over tonight and taught a card word game, and had a strawberry short cake with us.

Steve Harris, the Horse Gentler cowboy has been hanging

26

around our home. He went to meet again with the Hopi tribe Rangers. He wants to help them round up the wild horses. It looks as though he might be able to start as soon as next month to go out on the range. Many months later when he began to round up the horses, he came back to our Prayer meeting and shared that it would have been easier if he had been a Shoe salesman instead.

We're leaving for ten days of Expedition with the Hopi youth to the High Sierra Mountains. Will and Randy and I took the kids to Bishop, California to Mt. Tom and Mt. Humphreys. We had the kids doing some rock climbing routes. When we got back to our campsite and called our new staff lady, from England, staying in our home in Hopiland, she said that the Hopi Police had come by our place because someone had called saying that we were not supposed to be there. When she had explained that we had been there for some years, the Policeman went away saying that it must have been a prank call.

Every time I drove into Flagstaff, I felt like my heart was being painfully squeezed by the color, green. The color of the desert grew on me, but it took some years for me to fall in love with it.

The Color green is a dagger to my soul

Going back to California is not easy. It is very green out in Gail's folks' home in Montecito, CA. The color green is a dagger to my soul while my home is in Hopiland. This morning, Kevin and Gail showed me their new house which they are totally renovating in Carpenteria. It hit me that there was a death of yet another dream; I may never have a house with a backyard in a nice neighborhood in a place where it is green. When we went to visit Mark and Pam Chevalier's new home with a pool for their kids in Orange County, my old stomping College town, it hit me again that I was going through a grieving stage. We will be in Hopiland for a very long time and we'll never have a house like that for our kids.

I counted the cost of going back to Hopiland. What a coward I was to wish that I could go back to work at CMC Rescue and attend a white men's Church with everyone else. I dreamed that a friend's mom was visiting us from England, in a two story home which was ours.

Our Winter in Hopiland

We have many beautiful icicles hanging from our house. The children are busy taking plastic trash bags out across the street to slide down the little hill with Quinston and the other children. Our water pipes in the bathroom in the attic had frozen and busted so we had to shut off our water. We were told that this house was built by a Church from San Diego many years ago for Daniel Schirmer and his wife, Amy. Probably, they had no idea how freezing it gets up here in the winter time. After two days of no running water, we had considered using the outhouse which still stood in our backyard rather than our toilets which were full.

It was so cold that I could hardly get out of bed to have my quiet time with the Lord. It was 5 degrees F. at 7 AM this morning outside. Finally, I found a spot by putting my red chair in front of

28

our wall gas heater and closing the curtain which I made for the hallway to keep the heat. Even with the heater at the lowest level and still almost freezing in the house, we were shocked to find our propane gas bill to be almost $400 in one month because of the poor insulation. The schools were cancelled all over the reservation and Naphtali went out and made a snowman in front of our house. It is so cold, and yet, our neighbor children are outside jumping happily on our trampoline which the children bought with their own allowances.

Poor Clover had the coldest room in the north corner of the house. With single pane windows and no insulation on the walls, she might as well have been camping outside in the snow. Even with five layers of blanket, she sometimes used to wake up with the frost on the edge of her blanket where her breath took place.

When we went to pick up the children in Hotevilla for Sunday School, I got stuck at Arnold, Michael and Alyssa's house because of the snow. I was glad that Will was there with his car to help me rock and push my Caravan and was able to get me out. We didn't have our Church van yet. As it turned out, this would not be the only time I would be stuck in that village. This village was very traditional, and therefore, the traditionalists would not allow any paved roads here. With snow and rain, these roads became mucky with slimy wet sand and dirt, making it almost impossible to drive around.

But, it seems that the Hopi and the Navajos seem to know how to drive in these road situations. Or, perhaps, they are wise in staying away from driving when it is necessary not to. Several years later, when I was still getting stuck in the village, and the Hopi men were so gracious, to come out with their shovels to dig the Church van out, I wondered whether they were thinking, "Oh, that dumb Korean lady is stuck out there again!"

The snow got so wild sometimes when we used to drive back home to the reservation from Flagstaff late at night. It felt like I could get hypnotized while having to look at the swirling of the snow in front of my eyes for a couple of hours in the dark with only my head lights shining on the snow. There were no street lights on this 100 mile stretch.

Ida Walking Bear Murdock

Someone told me to go visit an old retired school teacher named Ida Murdock on the same street as our home, living in a two-story. When I first knocked on her door, a little woman hardly taller than 5 feet in height came to the door and looked up and almost shouted, "Who are you?" By this time, all five or six of her dogs had gone inside and her three cats were also there. She said not all of the dogs were hers, but she feeds them all. I did not know until later that she would become one of my best friends in Hopiland. Once, I mistakenly called her Ida Running Bear and she got mad saying, "Running Bear is a man's name," and that her name is "Walking Bear." She had a temper in a fun kind of a way and joked with me constantly with such a sense of humor that I found her to be delightful. She was imaginative too. When we used to drive into

Flagstaff together, she used to tell me many things she saw in the clouds. She would gasp and say, "Oh, do you see that ice cream in the sky? Oh, there is a... Do you see?"

Later, as she got older, she began to lose her memory. So, she began to forget what we had sung ten minutes ago in the car. One day, we sang the American Anthem three times on our way back to Hopiland in between all the other old hymns. A couple of times at Walmart, she forgot that I was going to come back soon to get her where she was sitting. All of a sudden, I would hear on the loud speaker system, "Millie Toms, your party is waiting. Millie Toms, your party is waiting at the front register area," all through out the whole store. Then, I knew all the Hopis from the reservation knew that day that I was at the Walmart.

Ida told me that she begged her mother to send her to an Indian Boarding School in California when she was only seven years old. This was because her uncle had come back to visit and

31

told her of all the oranges she could eat in Riverside, California. Once, as a little girl, Ida heard a neighbor telling her mother that she was lazy for sitting around. Ida heard her mother defend her to this neighbor by saying, "Ida is going to be a teacher someday".

She did go to Riverside Indian Boarding School and did not come back to see her land until she was out of high school. She had lost her Hopi language when she finally came home and she had not become a teacher because she, as well as all the other Indian girls, was put into servitude to white families for training to become house cleaners, maids, or hair cutters after the graduation. Ida told me that she was brought out into the hallway of the Boarding School by the dorm mother to have a white lady check her out for employment one day. At first, the lady was saying that Ida was too small. The dorm mother told the lady that she ought to take Ida home and try her out because the Hopi girls are the best workers. Ida worked for that woman for three years.

There was no bitterness in Ida's voice. In fact, she always said that she was glad that she went to school to get an education. She later taught many grades and, after retiring, she still taught Music at the Hopi Mission School when I was teaching Art there. We shared the same cafeteria and I watched her teaching the children to march to her piano rhythm and taught the children to play the little recorder flutes and bang other percussion instruments to different beats.

Ida's aunt, Elizabeth White, was a famous sculptor and the author of the book, "No Turning Back." She was also the first professional Hopi teacher. It was her aunt who made her go to the University of Northern Arizona, to get her teaching credential. Ida said that she cried when she was first dropped off at NAU, but that she soon became friends with many other white friends who were so kind to her. Ida became the first Native American young lady to attend this University in Flagstaff, Arizona. Ida's brother, Oswald White Bear Fredericks, also became the co-author of "The Book of the Hopi" written by Frank Waters.

Only weeks after meeting Ida, she came to me at the Hotevilla church food and craft sale at the Community Center (we were trying to raise money to buy a Church van) and simply asked me whether I could pray for her. She said she was ready to go to the Hopi Clinic because it was beginning to hurt. She amazed me with her child-like faith. I did not feel spiritual at all so I gave out a simple prayer thanking the Lord for loving Ida and asked Him to touch and heal her. Well, she said by the time she drove down to Kykotsmovi village only 10 miles away, the lump on her neck was gone. Ida told me that she was healed. I am sure I was just as surprised as she was.

Ida then took us to the home of a Hopi pastor named Karl Johnson Nasewytewa, who had some kind of a cancer of the skin on his neck. Will and I anointed both Karl and his wife Louise with some oil and prayed for healing in his home.

It was one of the harder things I've done in my life, later, to take Ida into town, to sit at the end of her feet, as the Dentist yanked and pulled out all her bottom teeth for dentures. I felt so privileged to be able to hold onto her ankles and just pray for my dear friend. Even as she was moaning, after all her teeth were out, she stood up and shuffled her

Ida Walking Bear Murdock

feet over to the Dentist in his office in the back and thanked him, now toothless, for doing such a good job.

Several years later, Ida was brought back to Hopiland to live at her Aunt Elizabeth's house and later, to her own stone home after it was fixed up, with care-takers to watch her. What great joy it was to be able to go and visit her once again without having to drive almost six hours to New Mexico. The time came when she hardly recognized who I was or even knew my name, but God's amazing grace was upon Ida so that she was able to play almost all the old hymns on the piano even in her mid-nineties. Ida would even sing the second soprano and harmonize with me and she playfully pounded the alto parts on the piano with even some of the chorus echo parts.

Our lives on Third Mesa

Clover was busy taking care of the horses and Naphtali was busy baking a cake and I was busy preparing some dishes for a Thanksgiving meal at the Church. Johnny was busy all morning playing in his pajamas with his new Nintendo games, and Will was chopping wood outside to take to an inmate's mother. Loretta Preston called to say, "Happy Thanksgiving" and the Murphys came from Flagstaff. Mom Audrey also came from Phoenix. We had some Korean youth who stayed at our house, and we had a small birthday party for one of them and played some Korean games until 11:00 PM. It is really refreshing to see these Korean kids who are so child-like and almost like the Japanese cartoon figures in their expressions when they talk and play. The Hopi people seem quite taken by these youth and are amused easily with them.

Many ladies cooked and baked for the Church food and Craft Sale at the Community Center. It was a windy day, and our sign kept falling down by the highway. Unfortunately, we hardly sold any of our quilts or aprons we made. But, we still made $529.31 towards our new Church van. What an encouragement this was to the ladies as they said they had never made that much money before.

In visiting the different pastors on the reservation with their Christmas gifts, we also visited Marvin Yoyoki. Marvin said that Karl talked of us coming over to lay hands on him and that they also want to learn how to do that. A few weeks later, we were invited to teach a few hours of seminar at their church; almost all their members attended, including Pastor Karl. I marveled at God's hand on all these things because Marvin was the one who called us before we came to Hopiland and really questioned us as to why we were coming. Now, Marvin said he was still amazed at how we were able to move into the Schirmer house since no one else had been able to get into it for about 15 years. The Schirmer House had sat like a Sleeping Beauty castle all these years with all of Daniel and Amy's accumulated things. Also old quilts, books, slides, stacks of materials etc. etc. were piled up high in dust, mice dung and urine when we moved in.

There are three mesas (First Mesa, Second Mesa, and Third Mesa) in Hopiland, with several villages on each mesa. As I recall, these were the names that the Spaniards gave when they first came looking for gold and saw the mesas. They simply saw the first mesa as they came into Keams Canyon and towards Polacca and called it the "First Mesa." When they saw the second set of "mesas," which in Spanish means the "tables," the flat top mountains which are settled with the villages of Shongopovi, Mishongnovi and Shipaulovi, they named them "Second Mesa." The villages of Kykotsmovi, Old Oraibi, Hotevilla and Bacavi are in Third Mesa. Today, when I was looking outside, it all seemed very beautiful to me. The sky and the buttes all seemed the color of sweet tangerine.

It is April now and the Engelbert-Fentons are here from Park City, Utah. Mike and Kathy, Luke and Leah, all walked with us across the street. Our neighbor's daughter had her baby and it has been twenty days since the baby was born. And now it is the day to have the "Baby hair-washing ceremony" with all the families and friends. They will show the baby to Dawa, the Sun, Father, for the first time.

I can see the dark rain clouds as I went up to the Church to join the weekly ladies' sewing time. We have been making quilts and aprons to raise funds to purchase a van for our Church as it was

35

getting more difficult to pick up everyone in my small Caravan and Will's car. Once I was cozily sitting inside, we could hear the wild winds shaking everything outside and bringing thick drops of rain. A couple of the ladies left saying that they had to go and cover the beans that are drying. The Hopis love to plant melons, beans and corn in their fields.

Marion Montoya called me this morning asking whether I could take her to the Hopi Clinic. She had two teeth pulled out this afternoon. Naphtali said that she did a movie critique and that it will be published in the Hopi High school newspaper. Clover has dropped her Spanish class and signed into the School Year Book class; she said she got to work in the photography dark room.

Sometimes, it takes everything in me to go up to church. It was out of total obedience just to go, because Will was going out to Flagstaff and it was snowing again. I went to build a fire at the church early since no one was there to open it. I thought I might sit in church all by myself, but Dynicea showed up and then, Arnold, then Michael and Alyssa and later Sylvia was the only adult who showed up. But, I believe today was important just to obey.

I am home alone now. The children have gone with Randy Nyce, a youth pastor out here, to the Zuni reservation to be in the Bible Quiz competition. Will has gone cross-country skiing with Barry, Rachel's grandson from the Bacavi village.

The kids are off this week for Spring break. Although there is much spiritual warfare in this land, my children are being blessed. They quickly were caught up with all their school work after being gone for two weeks in California. John won some school awards for his writing, all three are on the honor roll, and Naphtali has written some beautiful poems for school which show honor to God, and her faith. God has also blessed Will's heart, physically and spiritual; he had been complaining for awhile that he was feeling pain around his chest.

I cannot recount all those who have entered our home since we've been here over the past three months. Our small congregation is not growing because the people do not know who Christ truly is and therefore have a lack of commitment in their own hearts. One cannot tell who knows the Lord and who does not. However, it has never dawned on us to doubt our coming. It is not up to me to change their hearts and minds. All I need to do is to speak His words, and live as He would have me.

The sand in our door knobs

The wind picked up so badly this afternoon that my head and even my underwear seem to be covered with sand in a very short time just to get to my car. I am overwhelmed by all of the dust in our home from the sand, and also because of the ash from black coal in our stove. The sand comes in through every nook and cranny. It is even in our key holes in the door knobs so that we cannot open the doors with our key. Once, a small pile of sand dropped to the ground when Will took a door knob apart to fix it. Will said I need to imagine that we are living right on the beach with the ocean further out. I thought, "Yes, way, way out, somewhere over the Rainbow".

The Tumble Weeds and the Bull Heads

Will and John burnt some piles of the dry Tumble weeds around our home. We did now know to weed our yard diligently at the beginning when they first sprout all over our yard. They are deceiving in that they look so green and healthy at first; one would believe them to be beautiful green plants. But, soon, one will find out that they dry up and turn into huge tumble weeds which probably spread their seed all over as they tumble away. The bull heads have very sharp thorns which will stick to the bottom of everyone's shoes and are very painful to step on with bare feet. Whereas, I wondered why so many Hopis were out weeding these precious green plants when we first came, now I am also out weeding for many hours.

Traditional Hopi food

It was good to sit and eat the traditional "Nuquivi", a hominy (shelled corn) stew with mutton (sheep meat) along with the Hopi's outside oven-baked bread. The "Piki" bread, made in their Piki houses, is also served at all dances and ceremonies. It is an acquired skill, with bare hands, to paint on the blue corn meal batter onto an ancient stone and cook it so thin that it looks like a very thin Japanese rice paper which is then rolled carefully into a Mexican burrito shape.

The bread is cooked on top of an ancient stone handed down from their mothers to the daughters. A small fire has to be kept up underneath the stone all day and sometimes for many days. It has to be a work of love, even a prayer, as when one is angry or bitter inside while making the Piki, the batter does not get baked right and does not peel off easily and can sometimes rip. After a long winter, the first time Piki bread is made, one could get a blister from the hot stone from none-calloused fingers. The children eat the breads like they are candies. As this Piki is a staple food for the Hopis as bread is to the Europeans, we have used Piki in our Communion with Hopi Sweet water instead of crackers and wine.

Bleeding ulcer at Hopi High School

We enrolled our three kids into Hopi Jr. and Senior High School today. We had home schooled them for a year and a half and we were pathetic at it. The kids were too lonely; and so they prayed and felt that they were all to attend Hopi Junior and Senior schools.

Even though I felt peace this morning and even an encouragement from the Lord, I almost felt sick to my stomach this afternoon. Would they be okay? After all, did we not hear that the son of the last white minister in a certain village had been taken by an ambulance several years ago and was found to have a bleeding ulcer from going to this school? This minister and her son left the reservation six months after we arrived. But, before he left, this young man had told us that the kids were being cruel to him and that he could not even tell all the things which were happening to him at Hopi High because he did not want his mom to worry. Oh, this was almost as hard as coming to Hopiland itself!

This morning, I drove the kids to Hopi High. The girls ran out before I could stop them, but I did get to give John a kiss.

After teaching at the Hopi Mission School, I came home and anxiously watched for our kids to come home on the yellow school bus outside. We had a family assembly as soon as they got home and talked. We were so happy to hear that the kids at Hopi High were friendly!

200 miles for One Singer sewing machine needle

Will and I have to drive out to Flagstaff at least every other week, a 200-mile round trip each time. This time, our trip was because my Caravan needed three new tires. Other times, our trip involves purchasing bulk groceries, nails, a sewing machine needle, or going to the public library etc. Once when I broke my sewing machine needles and had no more, I could not finish my curtain project. I called everyone I knew, but no one had the right needle. I sat and cried thinking that I had to go 200 miles round trip to get this one needle so that I could finish this project. It is an exhausting day going to Flag as one can hardly stop to simply enjoy time in town because of the normally long "to-do" list.

Another Korean amongst the Hopi

I went to visit a couple in another village today. The wife, "Sim" is a Korean friend. She married "John" while he was in the

Air Force stationed in Korea. It was so strange to go into their home in Hopiland and see the beautiful, tall Korean armoires with abalone shell ornamental designs, in their living room. She came here over thirty years ago when this place was even more desolate. She told me how she had arrived at the Sky Harbor airport in Phoenix, Arizona and was driven out to Hopiland in the middle of the night.

So, imagine the shock when she woke up and found this "America" in the stark desert place, in what seemed to be in the middle of nowhere. She did not speak English or Hopi. Her husband soon took off to go back to the service, leaving her behind with his family in Hopiland. It was a life she had never thought to live, in what she imagined as America. Now, she has beautiful Hopi/ Korean grandchildren.

Our own menagerie

Haus is our Australian Shepherd, given to us by the neighbors of our friends, John & Georgia Wiester back in California. As a puppy, Haus was dropped from the back of a pickup truck while riding with the kids. He was a reject, for they did not think he could be a working dog, because of a limp on one of his legs, so we brought him out to Hopiland with us. On the contrary to what was feared, he ran swiftly like a true sheep dog, not chasing sheep, but the cars and vans.

Today, he survived getting run over by my Caravan because he ran circles around my white vehicle so close that I did not see him. But, the second time, Haus had an accident, we thought he was dead. We had considered putting him to sleep, but our kids were wailing so hard that we had to put Haus in our van and drive him 100 miles to Flagstaff to get him into surgery which cost us several hundreds of dollars! And I always complained about pet owners who spent so much money.

However, almost as soon as Haus was healed, that confounded dog went dashing after the Mission School van like lightening once again. Now, Haus has a cast on one leg (right front) and stitches on his chest.

Our rez puppy, "Daisy" which crawled into our garage; she was all skin and bones and growled at us like a fierce dog

Daisy is a stray Hopi dog which crawled into our garage starving and our kids adopted her into our family. Both of our dogs have been staying inside most of the time. This is in spite of my refusal to do so since I am not very fond of animals, like most of the Koreans I know. However, one cannot help but to feel sorry for these creatures since the temperature is below freezing outside these days. No one seems to care what I think, but want these sandy, hairy dogs inside our kitchen.

And our two puppies are getting along well. I feel sorry, however, for our two horses, "Shoshone" and "Fire" (a pure-bred Arabian) standing outside in the cold and snow. Both horses were given to us by friends, out of the blue, and they are yet more stories of miracles of God's provision for us.

Our two kittens, "Missy" and "Tiger Lily" which we brought home from Marion Montoya's house, are turning out to be already beautiful cats. However, they are quite a nuisance. They have wet not only our mattress, but the sheets I had just washed.

What life is about? How much is too much?

I received an advertisement from the Country Home magazine with the pictures of lovely country homes surrounded by

41

beautiful gardens. And all of a sudden, I felt a longing that went so deep into my heart that I wanted to cry. How is it that I wish I could have a house like that when I very well know that I am only passing through this earth? I am just a Pilgrim. Should I ever or would I be content sitting around in a garden when the Lord has called me to the desert?

This was a tragic day because Will and I got into an argument over an antique doll pillow which I refused to return to J.C. Penny. How it became such a big ordeal, I don't know, but it did. It was very sad - our stupidity! And, here I thought that I was marrying a quiet man, and perhaps he thought he was marrying some "Cherry blossom Japanese Geisha" like girl who would always say, "Yes, master," and walks ever so daintily like a little duck and gets him his slippers, and does not have an opinion of her own.

I wanted to feel like a Princess and Will wanted to be practical. (He is not always practical when it comes to buying books and mountaineering things though, which he says are for his work.) It seemed there was no remedy this time because we both stuck to our own thinking, and yet the Lord was merciful to us.

What is life about? Are we to abandon all liking for the material things of this world? After all, did not the Lord give us the colors of the red Roses and the beauty of white lace and the virgin snow? Would it be better not to have anything at all of earthly possessions? The envy in one's heart and the bitterness of not having may not be any better or noble either. How much is too much?

Should I wear pretty things on the reservation when most of the people dress simply? There was one lady I knew back at our Church in Santa Barbara. She always had a pretty or an interesting outfit and often wore a hat to our Sunday services. I could tell that her dresses were not always new or expensive, but she brought sunshine and joy to this earth. Life can be so mundane, and I felt

42

that she had tried to usher a bit of sunshine to our Church with her personality. When I went back many years later to share at our Church service, I saw that she was plain as everyone else and I missed the colors and the variety.

Today, I had a chance to re-decorate our hallway with the old pictures which Will's mom gave me on our last trip to Phoenix. I also re-organized the kitchen closets. This is also what life is about — the mundane things. I am sipping my cup of Chamomile tea in my "Enjoy the Gardening Season" tea cup set. It is silly but I like the clinking sound of the tea cup as I put it down on my little saucer. No man could enjoy such a thing, but it must be a pleasure thing the Lord has placed in the hearts of the females.

Lynda, Ginny, Janey, and Sharon drove all the way from Flagstaff just to spend time with me. I had a hard time accepting it for it seemed too much of a bother for them to have come to see me that far. But, the Lord tugged at my heart to accept these ladies as a gift from Him rather than feeling unworthy. Besides, I had no choice. We had a picnic lunch outside in our backyard and laid down with our heads together looking up into the blue Arizona sky. Two black crows flew over us. Lynda read a story to us. We listened to the Operas of my choice and had a tea party with some of my English tea pots and tea cups.

I never saw a field of Heather as in the book of "Wuthering Heights." But, I saw a pot of an absolutely beautiful bouquet of Heather, full in bloom, at Trader Joes. It was so beautiful that it almost took my breath away. I wanted so much to bring a pot home so I could watch it in my own living room, but it was a bit costly. How blessed a girl would be to grow up with a field of Heather!

I was watching a Midas car commercial. They were showing a desert scene that reminded me of the Hopi desert. My heart was sad because I couldn't love it. My heart sank wishing for a home in a beautiful green countryside with rolling hills and a creek running

43

through it.

It was much later that after going to a YWAM base in Texas where it was so green that I would realize how much I wanted to go back home to the High Desert in Hopiland.

Oh, Lord, heal us!

Oh how I hate our sin nature! I hate not understanding one another. Oh, Lord, will you come? Come and heal us. Help us to see you. Forgive us. Our prayer meeting was hard this morning. Once again, Will and I were in need of the Lord's kind mercy in our differences. Why is it so hard for Will not to get ready until the very last minute and why is it that I am so bothered by it? Could it be more than just our own battle of flesh and blood? My prayer is that we fight against the enemy and not against each other

Blessed is he whose Transgression is forgiven,
whose sin is covered.
You are my hiding place, you will preserve me from trouble;
You shall surround me with songs of deliverance.
Psalms 32: 1 & 7

Tonight, a Navajo evangelist Billy Lee spoke at Tuba City Assemblies of God Church. He spoke of the man in the Bible, living by a graveyard, with a legion of demons inside of him. But, when that man SAW Jesus, Jesus took him and made him well. How Jesus can make us well also. I think we all have demons of our own that haunt us, but I know where I can get help, and it is in the person of Jesus.

I noticed that I have a hard time with intimacy. This may be because of the Asian culture or simply because of my fears of being let down in some way. Sometimes, I found that I could only let people get so close to me emotionally, and then no more. I have made up my mind that I will no longer live that way. Without being unwise, I want to love on people and try to understand where they are coming from. I want to live this life fully and not always fear the outcome. I believe I am able give my ALL to Jesus and not hold back any part of me, perhaps, because I know He won't let me down.

This day was difficult for me. I woke up with Will to see the children get ready for school. We had our devotion time of singing and praying with the children. What an amazing privilege it is to be able to train them up in the way they should go in the Lord. How precious are these moments which engrave the mighty Word of God into their hearts and bless them in prayer! However, once the kids left, I went back to bed, believing that somewhat of a depression was involved. I slept until noon, which I have never done before.

December in Hopiland

Christmas is over and things have slowed down a bit. Havilah, an Amish gal volunteering at the Hopi Mission School spent Christmas with us and she is in our living room writing in her journal as we listen to Mozart.

Tonight, Sunday School children came to sing at the "Day of Prayer" (gathering of all the churches in Hopiland), held this time at the Polacca Baptist Church.

The new pastor couple and their three sons from Bacavi came over this afternoon to meet our family and stayed for a quick Lasagna dinner before we rushed off to the service. How we are still amazed at this team of friends that God has given!

At the Sunday evening service, Pastor Daniel Quimayousi looked discouraged. Uberta told me later that he told the ladies (there are no men who come to church) that he will no longer pick them up for Church when there is a ceremonial dance in the village, and that they could walk to Church. He would often find no one when he would drive around when Dances are held in the village.

Last night, I saw the largest snowflakes I had ever seen coming down. This morning, the land was covered in a blanket of white snow. However, the temperature was almost 40 degrees by late morning and all the snow melted. This should be good for our field that was plowed many weeks ago. We thought we would try the Hopi dry farming method where they don't irrigate but pray for the rain. It has been awhile since our family has been alone together. Tonight, the kids are doing their homework and watching a video about "Lewis & Clark." What an adventure! We are having one, too!

A Territorial spirit

John (Doo-Hoon), a Korean Methodist pastor, came to the church this morning and we invited him to our house for lunch afterwards. He brought packaged noodle soups and Kim-chee (a traditional Korean pickled cabbage) as gifts to us. He used to serve elsewhere with the Native Americans on another reservation, but he said his Korean Church denomination told him to come to Hopiland. He was a few years younger then I was, so he used to call me, "Noo-na" which means "older sister" in Korean. He used to drive back and forth from Flagstaff. He ended up being killed in a car accident some years later and was buried in the grave site at the Hopi Mission School.

We had another Korean Pastor show up to our house. He was from, yet another mainline Church Denomination. Soon, this other Korean Pastor told Doohoon to find another reservation to work on as he believed that his Denomination was in this land first in our village about fifty years ago. We could not believe the nerve of this pastor who was telling Doohoon to leave. We hate this territorial spirit which is already prevalent in Hopiland as there are many land disputes. Eventually, he, himself ended up going elsewhere when he could not get anything started.

"We're not responsible for our fathers' sins"

We have heard people say, "So, the Native Americans have had their land taken away, but what does that have to do with me? I don't want to apologize for something I have not done. That is in the past and I don't want to hear about it. There have been many injustices towards all human beings and all ethnic groups. So what? I don't want to hear the facts. The Native Americans need to get over it and move on."

In an individualistic society, we may say that we are not responsible for the sins of our fathers. And there are many Scriptures which would let us believe that when we confess our own sins that He is able to love and forgive us. And yet, there was King David who repented of King Saul's broken treaty with the Gibeonites.

There was a famine for three years. Year after year, David sought the Lord, and the Lord said, "It is for Saul and his bloody house, because he put the Gibeonites to death." David, then, called the Gibeonites and asked them, "What should I do for you and how can I make an atonement that you may bless the inheritance of the Lord?" David gave the Gibeonites what they asked for. It is not a pretty story, but afterwards, God sent the rain. (II Samuel 21: 1-14, Joshua 9) Thankfully, David had the wisdom to seek God and then reconcile with the Gibeonites because of the broken treaty. This brought healing to the land and ended the judgment of God.

It is understandable that we are somewhat at a loss as to what true Reconciliation would be with the Native Americans. I would like to give you an example. If I have slapped someone and beat someone up very badly, I would imagine that that person's children and grandchildren would always think badly of me. They may even think badly of my children and grandchildren if we lived in the same town. However, if one of my children went to one of the victim's children and said, "What my mother has done to your mother was uncalled for and it was a terrible thing. And I am truly sorry about what happened back then and I am sorry that it caused you much sadness in your family." This may be the beginning of a healing process.

However, it was just not one person or a few that this was done to. All the Native American tribes have been almost or completely decimated, raped, and their children taken forcibly to Boarding schools so that they were not able to be families. They were also stripped of their culture, language and dignity -- we have so much to reconcile. And this is not to bring a guilt trip, but only to bring awareness, which may eventually help to bring one healing at a time for this nation.

Some may say, "Our nation is founded by those who get themselves up by the boot straps and if you can't, it is only your fault." However, there are things we cannot begin to understand and the problems are very real even generations later. Could we pray for one Native American person or family at a time that the Lord would bring healing, joy, peace into their lives and into their tribes?

Furthermore, beyond just the recognition and apology, if a friendship had begun to where continual love and care was shown, this would be a furthering of this reconciliation process. Just the apologies alone may be cheap and the Native Americans are weary of having to listen to so many apologies alone as it had become a trend to just unload guilt by many whites. Reconciliation must seek to find respectful ongoing relationship where possible. We must be "Pahana", true Brothers and Sisters, to those we seek to share Jesus with. Conversions alone are not enough we must bring the Kingdom of God.

Compared to a Rape

This may sound harsh, but I could only compare the Native Americans' story to a rape, where the perpetrator tells the victim that it was her fault. It may be argued that she was raped for she had dressed provocatively or that she was walking where she should not have been. And then, when that raped victim is still having many nightmares and suffers other consequences from the memory of that rape, the perpetrator and his relatives tell her that she needs to "get over it and move on".

Randy Woodley with Eagle's Wings Ministry said once, "Please don't tell us to 'get over it and move on' because that would be putting us back on the Trail of Tears once again." Our native friends, the hosts of our nation need our prayers, NOT our judgments.

"Corpus Christi is dying."

I am reminded of a dream that our California pastor friend, Billy Minter, had in which he heard the words, "Corpus Christi is dying." In Spanish, Corpus Christi, means the Body of Christ. Then, he saw a vision of four Native ladies in their tribal regalia dancing and praying for the Church. What does this mean?

In Will's first encounters with the Lord that led to us moving to Hopi, he had two dreams about the Church. In the first dream, he saw us as the Church all together in a bus. He then, in the dream, confronted the bus driver asking, "Who are you, some kind of a cult leader?" Upon waking he asked the Lord what that was about and received a one word answer, "Bewitched." Galatians 3:1-3 says, "O foolish Galatians! Who has bewitched you that you should not obey the truth.... Did you receive the Spirit by the works of the law, or by the hearing of faith? Are you so foolish? Having begun in the Spirit, are you now being made perfect by the flesh?" Is Jesus leading the Church or is there something else going on?

49

In his second dream, he saw us as the Church all dressed up in our business suits. The Lord said to him, "Yes, you look good – but you have killed the Child." In Matthew 18:3, Jesus said, "Assuredly, I say to you, unless you are converted and become as little children, you will by no means enter the kingdom of heaven."

Before coming out to Hopi, about a year into the two years of dreams and visions, our Cherokee friend Phil, back in Santa Barbara, told Will of a dream he had. He saw the Church, as a crying white baby helpless on a high ledge of a desert butte. Next to the baby was a pool of water, representing the Holy Spirit, which it could not access. Down below on the desert floor was a Native American whose mission it was to make the difficult passage up to rescue the baby. We believe that the means of our rescue as a Church is full reconciliation with Native America. We believe the difficult passage for the Native peoples is to forgive us.

The following year in 1996, just months before we moved to Hopi, there was a *Promise Keepers* gathering in Atlanta. In preparation for this historic meeting of 50,000 pastors and elders, hundreds of Native American leaders walked a portion of the Cherokee trail of tears back into the city. We heard that it was an amazing gathering. One of our pastors told us that he had heard a native man address the massive assembly that day. Our pastor heard this native man saying something like, 500 years ago they had 100 percent of this land, but, today they only have 2 percent. 500 years ago, they had millions of people. Today, they only have 2 ½ million. He told of how the Europeans decimated their people…. And yet, this native leader said that he wanted not only to forgive them, but more than that, wanted to thank them for bringing knowledge of Jesus. According to our friend who had attended the conference, the whole stadium of Christian leaders broke down weeping, and repenting.

What is the answer to our failure with the Natives of this Land? Matthew 18:4, 5 says, "Therefore whoever humbles himself as this little child is the greatest in the kingdom of heaven. And whoever receives one little child like this in My name receives Me." We believe that our country, the United States of America and the Church stand on a foundation not of Rock but of Sand, in that unlike David we have never sought to fully deal with the sins of our fathers. We prefer, for the most part, to keep our heads comfortably buried in the sand. God have mercy on us! Father, please help the Native Peoples of this land to forgive us for our historical crimes and our present ignorance regarding them.

"How long are you staying?"

Will sometimes tells people of our first years with the Hopis, when they would ask him, "Who are you? Why are you here? and, How long are you staying?" He thought they were asking how long are you staying because they wanted us to leave. He came to realize however that they were really asking, "Will you stay long enough to be a true friend to us?" At its root that seems to be the meaning of the Hopi word "Pahana", that is True Friend. They have prophecy saying that Pahana will return to them and show them the way to the heavenly Father. This is a key to Native American mission work.

God Speaks Native American

"But, now ask the beasts, and they will teach you,
and the birds of the air, and they will tell you.
Or speak to the earth, and it will teach you,
and the fish of the sea will explain to you.
Who among all these does not know that
the hand of the Lord has done this,
in whose hand is the life of every living thing
and the breath of all mankind?"
(Job 12: 7-10)

"He shall cover you with His feathers, and under
His wings you shall take refuge."
(Psalm 91:4)

"But to you who fear My name, the Sun [not Son] of Righteousness
shall arise with healing in his wings, and you shall go out and
grow fat like stall-fed calves."
(Malachi 4:2)

Many people think that the Native Americans worship the sun. Some may, but, if one asks the Hopi people, they would say that they go out before the sunrise to meet Dawa (the sun) to pray, not because they believe that the sun is God, but that it is the strongest manifestation of God's creation. They will tell you that they know that the Creator, who is much greater, is behind that sun and they are not worshipping the sun, but the Creator.

Feathers may not mean anything to the Europeans or to the Asians, however, feathers mean prayers to the Native Americans. The Hopi men tie "pahos", Eagle feathers, in the kivas and put them outside; many will see these sites where the sticks and branches with feathers tied at the end at certain places on top of the mesas. The Bible talks much about the earth. If we read all the scriptures concerning the earth, and quote certain verses like "speaking to the earth", one may be accused of being New Age. However, I don't think that our God is intimidated by these things. And perhaps, we as Christians should give more room to be more tolerant of Native American symbolisms (not to worship any other gods - definitely not!) and allow them to use their rich symbolisms, as the Episcopal the Catholics do. The Bible is full of scriptures with pictures and descriptive words which speak like a poetic Native American language. We could fill a whole book which would speak of God's creations and poetry.

Will in a pool of water by the San Juan River.
Almost the only way one can get to this place
is by going down the river on a raft.
It is a quiet place with Cathedral rocks and endless sky.
One can feel peace and serenity in this place.

Chapter 3

I Did Not Know How Hard It Would Be

I did not feel thankful at all when twenty children came to Sunday School. I felt that they had come just for the cake and ice-cream more than for the Word of God. It was not until I sat quietly before the Lord at home later that I had a great sense of purpose and hope. I don't need to say, "Please" and beg Him for anything as He is more eager to give before I even ask, for He cares deeper, much deeper about His children in Hopi than I could even begin to imagine.

My heart seems to know no comfort today. Uberta and I met in Church and wept together before the cross on the floor for almost an hour.

My struggle is often with myself and no one else. Unbelief, impatience with our children, Will and myself and the Hopi people, criticalness, and the fear of men causes me much grief.

I did not know how hard it was for a Youth worker, Randy Nyce, who had been on the reservation for two years already, until we went down together to a Worship Leader's Conference at a Vineyard Church down in Phoenix. David Ruiz, after a session, gave an invitation for people to come up front to get prayers. We saw Randy go up and no one had come to pray for him as they were so many people up there. After awhile, Will went and prayed for Randy. Randy turned around and hugged Will and sobbed deeply for a very long time. It was, then, I saw that those were tears of many disappointments and rejections and weariness.

Early in February, I felt as though I was fighting off a pesky spirit of infirmity all day long. I knew that I had the victory to win. I spoke out saying, "Get your hands off of me!" The Lord gave me the strength to get off of the bathroom floor. I was able to attend Pastor Karl's wife, Louise's, funeral service at the Orabi Church. I was able to get to the burial site to see the men put the dirt in a mound shape and put the flagstones and the flowers on top.

First thing in the morning, Lucille Namoki from across the street called saying that she wanted to go to Church. We went and visited Vera and she was so happy to see us. While we were in the Church service, one of the Sunday School girls came into the Church and frantically said that a young lady from First Mesa, "so and so" had just died. She was someone we had ministered to in Jail. She had several beautiful children. I announced the news and I prayed for her and her family as I was crying in front of the Church. Well, as it turned out, this was just a false rumor and it was so unfortunate for me to have spread this horrible rumor even further before checking it out. I had no reason not to believe this. I had to go back and retract my announcement to the Church.

I got a call from a Hopi sister early this morning. She asked me to go and visit her mother, Mary in our village. Apparently, one of Martha's (not the real name) granddaughters had lost her baby that same morning. When Martha saw me at her door, she came over and hugged and wept and I cried with her. Too many people have died already.

Tchaikovsky's Sleeping Beauty

Driving back from Keams Canyon, I heard Tchaikovsky's Sleeping Beauty on the radio. It was the music they played in the children's animated movie, "The Sleeping Beauty". The Prince arrives and kisses her, awakes her from her sleeping death and takes her hand and they dance together at the end to this music of Tchaikovsky's symphony.

All of a sudden, my eyes were blinded by my tears as deep emotions touched my heart for I knew this was the picture of Jesus coming to kiss the bride, this Hopi nation. How beautiful it would be to finally see the Hopi believers dancing with Him someday! The music kept playing and I couldn't stop crying as I drove, saying, "Oh, Lord, let this happen, let your bride, the Hopis and the Native Americans take your hand!" I saw a few people waving at me as they drove by as I was coming towards the Hopi Veterans' Center, but I couldn't worry about what they were thinking.

Pumpkin bread & Campbell soup labels

I asked the Lord to help me to plan my day for I did not want to miss out on what He wanted me to do again. "Bake pumpkin bread," was all He said for the morning. The girls helped me chop the big pumpkin and shredded it to freeze some and bake the rest. One loaf for the teachers at the Hopi Mission School, another for Ida, another for Fermina and a Bundt cake for Pastor Karl and his family who invited us to sit down for a dinner, and another loaf for Sim who came and shared her stories for three hours with me tonight.

Once again, I felt totally dependent on the Lord to lead us this day. What I should do, whom I should visit, and whom I should call is a partnership between the Lord and me. I called Sim and prayed together on the phone for her husband, John, and her children Kim and Jr. I baked much again and delivered a loaf to Rachel H. up in Bacavi and sang some hymns with her and prayed. I was able to pick up Julie and went searching for three different kids' homes and then visited with Norlene for our prayer time together.

Going into Flagstaff to do errands is mostly exhausting. We had seventeen places to go on our list. A hardware store, Post office, a grocery store, the Library, office supply stores etc. We had not realized how we had done one or two errands a day when we used to live in the city rather than having to do all the errands all at once.

Our living room and the kitchen was one mass of boxes and boxes of Campbell Soup labels. YWAM Denver team with Mark and Donna McGowan spent approximately 80 hours to separate and cut these labels to be able to send them in to redeem a brand new van for Hopi Mission School. These labels had been sent by countless Churches in U.S.

Ida walked over to our house with all of her five dogs and our Daisy and Haus were not very happy. I was focused on typing the Compassion USA board meeting minutes.

Fellowship with the Assemblies of God and the Lydia Fellowship

We used to have such sweet fellowship with all the other pastors and the workers in our home almost weekly when we first arrived in Hopiland. We realized very soon that the Assemblies of God Church was left out in our meeting as well as the monthly get together of all the churches called the "Hopi Day of Prayer." Will suggested in our meeting, "Why not invite the Assemblies of God?" They were not included by more conservative church leaders in the past. So, we were able to invite Dr. Arne and Marge Thompson, the Pastors of the Assemblies of God Church in Polacca. Dr. Arne also worked as a physician in Gallup. It was now complete to have their congregation at the Day of Prayer for they brought much joy in singing.

There was a whole gang of Lydia Fellowship ladies one day at our home. This was the first time I met Fern Noble. She was indeed a very noble Cree lady who truly became a prayer warrior for us later to come and to teach in many of our Discipleship Training Schools. She became the personal prayer intercessor for John Dawson who wrote the book, *Healing America's Wounds*, traveling to many nations to bring reconciliation messages and prayer as a Native American.

Scholarships and the sale of our Condo

Clover has graduated from Hopi High School and received a 4-year full Regent scholarship to attend Northern Arizona University. Later, when we drove to register, we realized that she needed to purchase the books and there were other costs. We did not have all the money needed with us that day. Without even us asking, the lady behind the counter told us that Clover may qualify for yet another scholarship upstairs through another department. Before we knew it, we were driving away from NAU with a $1,000 check from the office and an additional $500 scholarship per semester in the future to cover above and beyond all that she needed. I never forget how I couldn't stop my tears of thanksgiving as I was driving away from the University. The Lord provided as He had promised! He said, "Seek first the kingdom of God, and all these other things will be added unto you." (Matthew 6:33)

And there is another offer for our condo in Santa Barbara, California. How strange it is that it would not sell when we tried to sell for a year and a half before coming to Hopiland. It seemed everything else sold around us but not ours. I had even cried out to the Lord thinking that we had sinned in some way. But, the market was down then and we would have lost money. But, after two years, it is selling within a week when the market is very much up again. God knew best!

Ministries

The children are coming regularly now to Sunday School. How glad I am of that! I can finally plan Sunday School curriculum without worrying how many, if any, would show. Thank you Lord! Video night at our church tonight was very good. Luke, Jeremy and Nathan came and helped serve snacks and drinks, put extension cords from the generator of Uberta's garage to the church so we can show the video movie to the children tonight because there was not enough solar power otherwise.

Will sometimes picks up the children in the mornings because of the snow and mud, because I am afraid to get stuck since there are no paved roads in the village of Hotevilla. It is not because they cannot have them but because the traditionals in this village have voted not to have the white men's ways of paved roads, running water, or electricity. They have an ancient prophesy that the world will end if the Hopi give in to the white man's ways. The Hopi are praying for the world and are trying to hold it together.

Will left for two weeks of training. First, he went to the Christian Wilderness Leaders Conference in Colorado, near Denver, a brief visit to YWAM Cimmaron, Colorado, then to Colorado Outward Bound training on Canyoneering and Desert Travel. Will wants to take Hopi youth canyoneering in the future in order to enlarge their worldview.

Will was gone for the school bus training license. Hopi Mission School is in desperate need of a driver. It seems that they cannot find a Hopi man who does not have some kind of drinking problem or a jail record. Russ, Jim, and Will have all decided to get the bus license to help.

"Why Does it have to be Sunday?"

Video night and the Snack shop were started up at the Hotevilla Church. One day I was so discouraged that no children were coming to Sunday School. I was complaining to the Lord in prayer and He simply asked in my heart, "Why do they have to come on Sunday? Why can't you have it on another night when they can come?" He said, "Don't be religious. Why don't you do something fun with them? Show fun videos such as "Veggie Tales." Make popcorn and let them buy snacks with the tickets they earned from coming to church. Let the big kids manage the snack shop"

God is working even when I may think it is not fast enough sometimes! Today, for the first time in two years, two of my neighbor kids came up to the village of Hotevilla for the kids' Video Night. It seems that it took that long for me to win their trust. She wanted me to ask her mom if it would be okay for her to come to Sunday School with me now. Her mom said, "Yes."

Going to the medicine men

"Peter", an inmate who received Christ in Hopi Jail, had some kind of a stroke. His mother called the pastor in Polacca to come to pray for him at the hospital in Keams Canyon. Even though the pastor anointed Peter with oil and prayed for him, he did not get better, so they want to go to the medicine man. We know that God is Jehovah Rapha (the God who heals) but not everyone is healed. Peter's girlfriend, "Raina", accepted Christ while in jail also and had been attending church with her daughter for many months now. Hopefully, Peter and Raina will claim victory over this stroke and the devil's schemes to harm them.

There are so many spiritual battles here on Hopi. We gain victory over one battle, and lose another.

On this October day, I realized that there has not been a baptism in Hopiland for at least twenty five years or more. A fourth grader "Colton" has told his parents that he does not want to be initiated into the Hopi kiva doings, although many of his relatives have been coming around and asked him to do it. He told them that he wants to follow Jesus and be baptized. Colton's mom admitted tonight that his dad has taken Colton to a medicine man twice because of his desire to be baptized.

A Baptism, to a Hopi is a very serious matter. Hopis consider this the final act of betrayal, and they claim that the person is "ka-hopi", no longer Hopi, once someone chooses to be baptized. Whereas, the Baptism is simply an expression to announce one's faith in what Jesus has done on the cross and rose again, the Hopis have believed in the past, and in the present, that it is an announcement to everyone that he or she will no longer be Hopi. This is what the missionaries taught in the past.

Cross & Migration symbol petroglyph

Chapter 4

A Demoniac in Hopi Jail

Hopi Jail ministries have now started. While I was having a quiet time with the Lord, I heard a quiet voice in my heart saying, "Jail." Yes, I believe that God can still speak to us as He did with the prophets of old for He is the same yesterday, today and tomorrow. I was not interested in doing a jail ministry. Many of our friends went to do jail ministries back in Santa Barbara but I did not feel that God was calling us to do that then as we had my "Morning Glory ladies group" and YWAM ministries also. But, the next morning when He said, "Jail", I knew He wanted us to go to do the services at the Hopi Jail.

Before I lost my nerve, I decided to call the Jail. I called, and Captain Silas answered. He asked, "How can I help you?" When I asked whether we could come and do church services for the inmates, he asked what that meant. The Lord had already spoken to me about three things: One, Sing with the men and women inmates so they are worshipping and not being entertained. Two, Have the inmates read out loud the books of the Gospels together, so that they get hungry to read more. Three: Prayer.

The Captain asked me how often I would like to come in and I thought I was being generous by saying, "Once a month." He then said, "If you're going to come once a month, they are going to ask for you, so come once a week! And can you come, starting this Monday night?" I was so surprised that I said, "Yes," even though Will was gone on a long ministry trip. Pastor Daniel and Uberta and Heleen went in with me that Monday evening. Pastor Daniel said he used to go in many years ago. He said only two or three men would show up. We were all shocked to have over sixty men show up that evening. Pastor Daniel later said it was because of my guitar. We met for an hour with the men, and then an hour with the ladies.

I could hardly believe what happened tonight at the Jail. The inmates had taken turns and finished reading out loud the last three chapters in the book of Mark. Reading out loud is good, so that they can find out about the goodness of Jesus, for themselves with their own eyes and mouths rather than being spoon-fed. These chapters told of Jesus' resurrection.

One of the inmates had a demon manifestation. He screamed something out and threw the Bible across the room towards Will with the pages falling out. You could have heard a pin drop as all the men quietly watched with their wide eyes to see what would happen next. There was a spiritual battle in that room. Will spoke out some words slowly in tongues and his eyes were riveted to that young man's eyes. No one understood what he said, but it was a command. The young man sheepishly stood up and quietly left the room.

An Art Teacher

I was glad I started teaching Art at Hopi Mission School. The children are choosing between three different projects to work on at their own pace. They can paint helium balloons flying over anywhere around the world. Some have chosen to fly over dinosaur land or Disneyland, some over the ocean, others over a circus. Another project is to do a paintbrush dotted picture like "Monet". And last, they can build a Hopi village with the brown clay.

I have been teaching Art; grade K through 6th, at Hopi Mission School for the past two and a half years. The Heard Museum Indian Children's Art Show in Phoenix is now over (more than 80% of our children brought in ribbons), but the Hopi Art Show will be at the Hopi Civic Center for the next two weeks.

The Biggest church is in Hopi Jail

Again and again, I recognize that I don't have anything to give. I felt this way tonight for the jail ministry. I prepared the songs only moments before leaving for so many things had come up during the day. Marion Montoya came with us tonight. I believe that the Lord came in a gentle way as we sang and read Mark 14th chapter. The inmates took turns reading it out loud. A couple of them even asked questions and some stayed to shake our hands.

Daniel and Will met "Rick", a former inmate, and his father. Daniel had run into Rick at the village store on Wednesday and Rick had a lengthy conversation with Daniel about how touched he was by the jail services on Monday night. Today, Rick noted what a difference he felt between leaving his cell burdened down with oppression and how, after attending the services, he had returned again in peace.

Joe Rodriguez went with Will and me, to hold church services at the Hopi Jail. Every week we have 45 to 70 men. This was before they divided the room. We also have 10 to 15 women, all attending voluntarily. It is the biggest church in Hopiland, in that it is a gathering in Jesus name.

A Christian woman named "Sandy" is under great condemnation for the deaths of her three children. It is difficult for the Hopi to continue in their walk when others of their tribe are condemning them. Real conversion of the whole man is a challenging process here, or anywhere. We gave out to our prayer partners, 30-40 copies of the original inmate prayer photos, with their permission. This is an honor and a privilege because photo taking, video taping and sketching are not allowed in Hopiland. One will get their cameras taken away if caught. Now we have five more photos of three men who desire prayer

For the fourth time, the jail guards changed the visiting procedure so that we couldn't be consistent. They would only let us see the ladies the last time, so we thought we'd see only the men tonight, but they wanted us to split the time with both men and women. The inmates read the first chapter of the Gospel of John and we were once again amazed at their reception! God is moving.

Sicknesses and discouragements

I am feeling pretty awful and so incapable of being able to do anything good in Hopiland. I feel so out of it. I did not want to do the jail ministry and Will is gone doing a wilderness outing with Hopi youth leaders; I just wanted to rest. Today was a holiday from schools so the children stayed home. The wind was pretty bad and cold today. Naphtali is sick also. She is feverish and sweaty. I think she caught a flu that is going around. I also felt sick, hardly able to talk without discomfort.

I began to feel discouraged, feeling useless and depressed. God has done so much in such a short period of time, but when I am sick, it is hard to focus on the glorious plans of God.

My Friend Carol Odegaard who has been a Registered Nurse for many years in the Emergency Room at the Flagstaff Hospital said that she had never seen so many Hopis die as this past year, not from old age, but from accidents and sicknesses.

Tonight, my date with Will, which was supposed to have been our Valentine celebration, was not at all pleasant. If I had known how exhausted I was, I would have postponed our date. Tomorrow, Will is going to leave early to meet Fred Gomez, the youth leader at the Bacavi village center, and some of the Bacavi youth at Jack's Canyon for rock-climbing and a camping trip.

But, as for me, I will hope continually and
I will praise You yet more and more - Psalms 71:14,15a

Throwing up blood

I do not know what exactly happened tonight. I felt so nauseated all of a sudden that I had to vomit, but no food came out, but only some blood. I was covered with cold sweat from the top of my head to the bottom of my feet. I was moaning and found myself on our bathroom floor feeling so very sick

With Will being gone for two weeks, it is natural that the enemy would attack at this time. I am definitely not against going to the hospital although at this point we do not have insurance. Another thing is that many people are praying for me and if someone has put a curse on me out here, I want them to see that our God's medicine is stronger and my full strength will be regained because of my Savior Jesus Christ. The enemy lost! By 11:00 PM I sensed God's presence and felt something lift, and slept through the night.

Satan is always out to crush, kill, and destroy. He does not want us to have unity, so he attacks us even more when we are trying to attain that goal. He tries to sidetrack us and divert us from God's plans for our lives. He does not always directly attack us, but sometimes attacks our children.

Your God has commanded your strength; Show yourself strong,
O God who has acted on our behalf - Psalms 68:28

But, as for me, the nearness of God is my good;
I have made the Lord God my refuge
That I May tell of all your works- Psalms 73

Witchcraft and Curses

Will and I have noticed that some of the Hopi culture is saturated in witchcraft more than we had realized. Witchcraft simply is trying to manipulate in the spirit realm what goes on in the lives of human beings, animals and the things on this earth.

Since we've been back from our trip, a young man came over to our house. When I asked him whether his dad was home, he said that his dad went to visit a Medicine man. The reason for this was that someone had killed their horse with two gun shots at 2:00 AM. Now, their father went to speak to a Medicine man so the same kind of evil deed can be returned to the one who did this to them.

Hopis go to the medicine man for many reasons. One lady who has been attending the Church faithfully for months now since she came out of the Hopi Jail, said that she took her boy to a medicine man in Polacca. He had fallen and hurt his leg. The Hopi Clinic had such a long waiting list that they couldn't do anything about his swollen leg. The boy was completely healed by the medicine man's treatment. However, this last Sunday, the same woman came to church instead. Regarding this we know a medicine woman who heals joint injuries and gives the credit to God only, not her own powers or other spirits.

Horse Accidents

While out riding our Arabian "Fire," with Will, our daughter Clover was injured. Will said that when she hit the ground she looked up just as Fire got spooked and kicked back. Her riding helmet was cracked all the way through inside. Her forehead had a good gash that looks like a "Frankenstein" scar. It is a miracle she lives. She did not take on the spirit of fear and wanted to ride the horse again this weekend.

It was later, another time, that I also had a very serious horse accident. I remember lying on the sandy ground where I had been

caught in between the two horses and got kicked many times at full kicking force. It was in the evening and I could see so many stars in the sky. As a Hopi elder friend sat next to me on that sandy soil, while Will went to call the ambulance, a prayer came out of my mouth, "Oh, I praise you Lord, for this beautiful evening with all the stars you have created. I thank you for my life and that you have protected me..." Then, when I was finished, I heard this elderly man also say a prayer in Hopi and English. He finished the prayer in the name of Jesus, even though I did not know him as a believer in Christ. I know that I could have been easily killed that night or paralyzed, but the Lord saved me.

The ride in the Ambulance was almost more painful than the accident itself as I was bound to a hard board like a mummy to prevent anymore injury and my whole body and head ached like I was being tortured. We had to go almost 45 miles to Keam Canyon Hospital (this was before the new one was built near Polacca) and it was almost an hour away.

Being alert at all times

The horse accident happened because we were too casual at the end and not alert when I was getting off of the horse. We need to finish the race well; we need to not lose our sight. We had seen that a "Pecking order" was being established between our big Mustang and the horse we had borrowed. Steve Harris, the Horse gentler, tried keeping "Shoshone" our Mustang from kicking the horse I was riding all day and away from Clover who was on our other horse, "Fire". When we had come back to our destination, I casually got off to put the horses in a barn and that is when Shoshone quickly turned its rear and started kicking

I need to be like the 300 soldiers of Gideon who lapped water when they got to the Jordan river. (Judges 7: 1-9) It was not enough to be valiant soldiers - 22,000 of those who put their faces to the river to drink were sent home! They were not fearful or afraid, but they were too casual in the war, and were disqualified..

A Rattle Snake in our Yard

When hearing about the rattlesnake in our front yard and Clover's injury, one Hopi Christian lady said that we have to be very careful out here because, "We are a wicked people with much witchcraft." I wasn't sure if she was warning me of some curse put on us or not. In almost ten years of living in Hopiland, we saw only two rattle snakes on our property.

Once when I was sitting on our couch in our living room, I saw something moving in my Apple tree outside. It was a Garter snake which had somehow crawled up the trunk of my Apple tree

and coiled itself on its branches and then started unwinding itself
and hanging straight down with its pretty designs on its body. I felt
like Eve in the Garden of Eden. However, I did not talk to this snake
and change the course of history of the human race.

Another time, when I came home in Kykotsmovi, a snake
was blocking me on our first step going up to our front porch. It was
all stretched out literally the whole length of the step. I shuffled my
feet and it slowly slithered away. Another time, another snake was
stretched out just in front of our front door.

We found others snakes in our
garage and in our home a few times.
Some Hopis say that someone is trying
to curse you when you find a snake in
your house, and become fearful. Some
say that a Medicine man needs to be
called in to cleanse your place so that
nothing bad would happen to you or
your family. However, the Scriptures
are so powerful and give me such
strength during adversity. After these
happenings, I reminded myself of the

*A Dead rattle snake in our
yard*

Scripture verse, "Greater is He that is in me than he that is in the
world."

Because you have made the Lord, who is my refuge
Even the Most high, your dwelling place,
No evil shall befall you,
Nor shall any plague come near your dwelling,
For He shall give His angels charge over you
To keep you in all your ways,
In their hands they shall bear you up,
Lest you dash your foot against a stone,
You shall tread upon the lion and the cobra,
The young lion and the serpent you shall trample underfoot

Because she has set her love upon Me,
Therefore I will deliver her,
I will set her on high, because she has known my name
(Psalm 91- *the 9-1-1 Chapter*)

A rock thrown into our Church

During the Sunday evening worship service on November 8th at Hotevilla Gospel Church, a large rock was thrown into the church. Uberta usually sits by the window to lead singing, but was not hit. We also had 16 children in the other room for the Video Evening. No one was hurt by this incident. Many Hopi Christians and the children who come to church are ostracized by their families and communities. Some kids and adults totally give up church due to this.

Hopi police for the second time

Today, November 14, I had to call the Hopi police for the second time since being in Hopiland. The first time was when we were doing the highway clean up with the Hopi Mission School.

This time, I called because a mother had been badly beaten and a 14-year old girl had been sexually abused by someone; our friend witnessed this and told me the next morning. Will convinced me that it was my obligation to report the abuse, even if it meant hurting a relationship with a good friend. If I did not, I would be contributing to our sick society here where everyone turns their heads as if nothing happened when a crime had been committed. Also, we cannot keep shielding and protecting our so called "friend" who did evil and harmed others. Recently this same young man had told Clover that he had fed marijuana to our horse.

Some of our staff and DTS students at "River House" on the San Juan River. There are amazing Petroglyphs on the rock walls which the ancient people left long ago.

Chapter 5

An Oasis in the Desert - A Garden

What I see in my front yard is amazing. Will and our children helped me put in a gated fence area so that the flowers and my trees can be safe inside my garden. Soon, there will be apple trees and many kinds of flowers and butterflies and hummingbirds. It will be an Oasis in the desert where people can come and know the love of God. Myrtis MacCormack came over and helped me plant two of my Peach trees.

I went to distribute the bags of food from "Operation Blessings" with Ida to her families and to neighbors. At her nephew's place, I was overwhelmed to see bunches of purple Irises. I did not know they could look so beautiful in the middle of the desert. I will plant purple Irises and roses in my garden as well. Ida let me dig a whole bunch of Iris bulbs from what was her Aunt Elizabeth White's garden which was a bit far from the house and not tended by anyone. I had no idea then, that these purple Irises would multiply ten fold in my garden at our Hopi house so that I was able to give them out to Virginia Yoyokie in our village, Juanita Yepa on the Jamez reservation and to my sister-in-law, Kathryn in California,

This is my wild garden in the desert (Rabbit Brush)

and to many others. These purple Irises were one of the first flowers to greet me in the Spring time, all around my garden, at our home in Flagstaff later.

A Pied Piper

I love the Lord who is so faithful! I came out of the church and the stars were so many and so brilliant! The Lord showed me today that if I am faithful with little that He is faithful with much! The Lord is working all things out! When I went to pick up the children in the village for Sunday School, I felt like the Pied Piper with his flute in Hotevilla. Everywhere I turned there were children screaming and waiting, and some parents were standing in their doors with their children as I came around the corner. A young father of one boy came out and greeted me with a big smile and a handshake and said, "I remember you from jail." It was a good thing another person was following me to pick up the children because she had ten children in her car after my van was totally full.

A dark figure in our kitchen

I sometimes sleep on the couch when Will is gone. I woke up in the middle of the night on the couch with a dark figure of a man standing in our kitchen and I could see that his wide pants legs were slightly spread apart. He stood very still next to our cutting board and his stare was so piercing and eerie in the dark that I was completely frozen in my ability to scream or even to breathe. I felt it

A Petroglyph of a benevolent spirit?

was someone we already knew. Finally, I was able to pretend that I was turning over slightly and murmured, "Clover, are you awake?" Clover murmured something back from the other couch.

I felt that it was safer to ignore him rather than confronting him and hoped now that he knew I was awake that he would go out. But, the figure was still standing very still as I peeked over my blanket, which almost covered my whole face, and I desperately cried out to the Lord inside. What would happen next? The figure suddenly disappeared right in front of my eyes and what I thought were the pupils of his eyes were only the red light on our cordless phone mounted on our wall. What were just moments seemed like an eternity!

I do not usually get frightened easily. During my college days, I was able to calmly deal with a gun pointing right at my face with the gunman raging and cussing at me at the closing time at my work at a pizza joint. But, I certainly felt the lack of power that evening with that dark figure in our kitchen. A few days later, Melanie Cripe called from California, not knowing anything about the figure I saw.

It is not to say the following is what had happened. However, she shared how some missionaries had just come to her church from Africa and shared about a witch who had decided to do "an astral projection" with some other witches, to get out of their bodies, to go to the home of a missionary family, to murder them. However, when they got there, they found that the angels were surrounding the house and the witch could not get in. The witch later came to know the Lord as his Savior.

A terrible nightmare

I had a terrible nightmare. It was about a boy who kept sobbing and sobbing in my dream. Then I saw a man rise up with an evil smile out of mud or a rice field, holding a stiff frozen-like chicken. However, I was terrified to see that the frozen chicken was that same boy who was sobbing. Will and I prayed for an interpretation. We believe that Satan wants to kill the Hopi youth before they rise up to be men of God. We need to pray all the more diligently!

Time together with the other missionaries

Even in the midst of the chaos of the wind outside, we sat united and cozy inside while everyone sang "Happy Birthday" to me in six different languages (Pastor Doo Hoon Jang in Korean, Joe in Spanish, Melanie in Tagalog, Daniel in French, Heleen in Dutch, Pastor Patrick (who is from England but lived in India) in Pakistani. They also sang, "I love you with the love of the Lord" in several languages. It was rather astounding to see this many nations represented on this small Hopi reservation, right in our small living room.

We had our Wednesday morning pastors and missionaries prayer meeting at our home today. A young missionary woman hid her face behind her husband and cried and cried. We just held our breath. They have only been married for five months. Two months ago, they came to help Uberta at the Hotevilla Gospel Church and are living with her. The wife said she knew it would be hard to live here on Hopi but not this hard. We all gathered around them and prayed. The young couple left within a couple days.

On this March day, the wind was howling and blowing sand around so fiercely that it created a sand dune right in front of our door again. Although the wind is sometimes compared to the Holy Spirit, the constant howling of wind on this reservation for days can almost seem demonic and make one feel as though one can go mad. The howling is almost like the desolate cry of a wolf pack.

Even if one may have a desire to work in Native American ministry and feel called, it is not easy to stand up to all the oppression and isolation. During the winter, it might be comparable to "cabin fever." There is such spiritual oppression and heaviness here. Even many Hopi find excuses to run into town (Flagstaff, Winslow, or Tuba City) just to escape the spiritual climate on the Rez. Sometimes, one can feel the spiritual oppression as one is driving into this nation.

I should not be discouraged when everyone cannot be here for the Pastors' prayer meeting. It is so easy for me to judge when I think they are putting other work before prayer. When I said that they should skip doing some work, Pastor Patrick from England said to me, "It is because you are an Evangelist and we are Pastors." I never even thought of myself as an Evangelist before. I should take the log out of my own eyes before trying to take the speck out of their eyes. I felt lonely today even with all these people around. I should go out and make a garden.

The Murphy's home

Jim and Celine Murphy's home in Flagstaff is a haven! The Murphy's guest room, their "Prophet's Chamber" is nicer than any motel. How we love this couple whom God has provided for us. They were holding weekly prayer meetings in their home for the Hopis years before we even moved out to Arizona. So, when Will came out to scout out the land and met them at the Hopi Day of Prayer at one of the churches, the Murphys invited him to sleep overnight at their home afterwards. And we have been there often when we needed time away from the reservation and were too exhausted to come home after all the shopping and the errands in town. They have been like loving surrogate parents to us. We have always been able to go to them for so many prayer requests.

Sedona and Oak Creek

Climbing roses were everywhere in Sedona among many other kinds of flowers. Sedona is 2,000 feet lower in elevation than Flagstaff. It is these flowers I noticed and not so much the red rocks; they didn't mean anything to me then. It is strange how certain things and places grow and get lodged in a person's heart, to make the person who she is, for I would come to be very fond of these red rocks later.

Oak Creek in Sedona is such a wonderful place. I had a pond of my own with grass reeds and green trees all around and above me. Our three kids took floaties and played by small water falls. They are no longer little anymore, all teenagers now. I would close my eyes and open them and my sight was set not on an imaginary, but on a vivid beautiful green world! It was very nice to be able to be with just my family, to rest, play, sit by the fire, and to go to sleep in a tent together.

We found another spot that was so picturesque that I could not have asked for more. Will made Ginger Corn bread in the Dutch oven this morning. After playing catch, we spent some time to sit in the Creek. The water was quite cold but everyone except me went swimming. John found a couple of water snakes and Clover and I found a pretty nasty looking centipede falling into the water.

The town of Sedona is known for being one of the seven spiritual hot spots of the world amongst the New Agers. Once, I was sitting on the red rocks, looking out at this beautiful country when a young gal came down and stood in front of me. I had run into her some minutes before. She had a scarf over her bald head; it seemed she had chemotherapy recently. I believe that she thought I was a Native American for I had some turquoise earrings and bracelet. Many New Agers are into Native American religions. So, she asked me, "Ma'am, do you happen to know where the vortex is?" I looked at her stunned for a second and responded saying, "Young lady, the vortex is right here in my heart and His name is Jesus. You should get to know Him!" Now, she looked at me with a stunned look and the only thing she could say was, "Oh, yes, ma'am!"

"Workaholics"

I stayed at my mother's place in Southern California, while Will and the kids all went with my brother Daniel and his wife, Kathryn, and their son, Westin, to sleep over at their home. All morning and afternoon, mom and I worked and cleaned. Mom couldn't just make a dozen or two white Chinese stuffed rolls, but had to make enough to feed an army. Mom and I talked about why she and I both seem to have such an obsession to be workaholics. We didn't have an answer other than that it is an inherited thing. The town of Carlsbad was such a pretty little town as well as all those quaint beach towns on the way to San Diego.

Encouragements

God is moving! He wants to bring His good message of hope, and not despair, to these ladies, their families, and the Hopi villages. I was so excited by the turnout and event that I could not go to sleep until really late.

God keeps giving me encouragement. On Tuesday, a mother working in the store in Kykotsmovi asked whether I was picking up her child for the Video Night. Two other girls from my village came and also wanted me to pick up their friend in Old Oraibi.

This morning, our Wednesday missionary prayer group of eight people met, Pastor Uberta from Hotevilla taught us our first Hopi lesson. Although each village has its own dialect, the Hopi believe that Hotevilla has the highest form of Hopi language, so Uberta is the best teacher available.

God is working even when I may think it is not fast enough sometimes! Today is October 11 and for the first time, two of my neighbor kids came up to the village of Hotevilla for the Kids' Video Night. It seems that it took that long for me to win their trust. I found that one has to be patient in this land. It is useless and vanity to be ambitious, to think that just because one thinks oneself charismatic in personality that things will happen fast.

Although this might not seem significant to others, for the children to attend church and other Christian events when their parents and family are not church-goers, this is incredible here.

Electricity someday soon

We may get electricity put in our Hotevilla Gospel Church in 1 or 2 years. Hotevilla is one of the most traditional villages in Hopiland, and the people voted once again this year not to have any running water or electricity. But the church is close enough to the street and the store on the boundary line where the electricity is allowed. Now the realty office will have to do archaeological research to see whether anything may be sacred, and then our application has to be signed by the village leader, and then by the Hopi tribe, and then to the Winslow office. God can do it!

"Puhu Qatsi" (New life) women's fellowship

A friend and a Counselor at the Hopi Guidance Center shared with me that God is moving in the Hopi Jail. She shared that an inmate has made a decision to follow Christ because of the jail ministry, and that this woman told her she feels it is the ONLY WAY and that what we shared was THE TRUTH. Although, our friend, as a counselor, cannot share Christ at her work place, she has been thinking about having some of these ladies come to her home in Kykotsmovi for a weekly sharing time and simple Bible studies.

We had our first "Puhu Qatsi" New Life ladies' fellowship in Kykotsmovi on October 15. Most of the women were in their 30's. I asked them what it was that they want from these meetings. We went around in a "talking circle" and they gave topics such as: Faith that things can change for the better, health and well-being, trust in God, being obedient, self-worth, getting away from self-pity, better parenting, forgiveness, release from fear, etc.

Yes! The answers are all in the Bible. The women shared and cried, and sang new songs to the Lord. Afterward, some women asked if they could bring their friends next time. Even if they never come back, we know that they heard the message of Hope at least this once. God is moving! He wants to bring His good message of hope, and not despair, to these ladies, their families, and the Hopi villages. I was so excited that I could not go to sleep until really late.

Our Thursday night ladies group has been named, "Puhu Qatsi," meaning "New Life." I wish I could send a picture of these beautiful Hopi ladies that are in our group. However, in Hopiland, taking photographs, or videos, or even sketching is not allowed. I want to respect that. Perhaps I can get permission from the ladies

A vision of the Koreans in Hopiland

Before coming to Hopiland, I was praying one day and God spoke to me in my heart so clearly and said, "Millie, your people will be a part of this adventure." I believe the adventure is that we will work together as in Isaiah 58:12, "Those from among you shall build the old waste places; you shall raise up the foundations of many generations; And you shall be called the Repairer of the Breach, The Restorer of streets to dwell in." I believe that the Lord wants to raise up an army of 200 Koreans to go out into the Native world, starting right here with the Hopi.

Two years ago, God gave me a vision during my prayer time before coming to Hopiland. This November, that vision came true. Hopiland had a chance to see the beautiful Korean drum dance, the spectacular fan dance, and other traditional dances held at the Hopi Civic Center. A thousand people filled the stadium. Three Korean pastors from Los Angeles brought this group out to perform in this 5-hour program. Even with the heavy snow, everyone stayed to watch.

The Tae-kwon-do Korean masters have been coming out to train about 25 Hopi young people, who gave demonstrations as well.

Hopi Jail

The following day, during Hopi Jail church service, I delivered art work from three Hotevilla children to their mom. The artwork was done at Sunday School yesterday. The beautiful pictures said, "Me plus God is a powerful team." We allowed the inmates time to do art work so that the mother could send hers back to her children. In her artwork, she said, *"God has given me a crown of beauty instead of ashes, the oil of gladness instead of mourning, and a garment of praise instead of a spirit of despair."* (Isaiah 61:3)

A Call for prayers for Israel

Today is a call for prayer and fasting about the Anti-Missionary bill in Israel. I received an e-mail from a Messianic congregation in the Tel Aviv area who informs me that presently the Anti-Missionary bill has been taken out for the time being. However, a Shas Party Knesset member is presenting a bill that will be worse than the former.

In the Penal Law, 5737-1977 1, following Article 174B will come: "Prohibition against preaching to change religion" 174C.

Anyone who preaches with the purpose of causing another person to change his religion is liable to three years imprisonment or a fine of NIS 50,000." This amount is approximately $14,000 in U.S. dollars.

The Island Breeze team for the Fourth of July!

What a treat it was to have our YWAM Island Breeze team come to Hopiland by the invitation of the Hopi Tribe! It was a strange way in which the Lord accomplished this. We presented the idea of bringing this Polynesian Dance team to come into Hopiland while they were already performing at the Sky Dome at the Northern Arizona University with the YWAM Impact World Tour earlier this year.

It became apparent that the Pastors did not feel comfortable with the Island Breeze team coming. We felt it would be so incredible for the Hopi nation to be able to see these beautiful Hawaiian and other Polynesian dances which glorified our Lord. All their dance outfits were beautifully made and none were provocative. They even have a "Resurrection Dance" which tells the story of our Lord Jesus. I had prayed for this team to come to Hopiland, and now they were so close in Flagstaff and I didn't understand why the Lord was saying not to bring them when we had the Veteran's Center reserved.

After praying, we chose not to bring division into our prayer time, but to relinquish the right to have the Island Breeze team come at this time. It was some months after the team had gone back home after their tour when Karen from the Vice Chairman's Office from the Tribe called us. She was asking whether they could have Island Breeze come to the first Fourth of July Celebration at the Hopi Civic Center for three nights. It was an amazing thing to watch how the Hopi Tribe paid and flew twelve of the Island Breeze members back out to Hopiland from Florida! Just in one night, there were over 3000 people at the Celebration.

At the Resurrection Dance, a story was being told from a loud speaker, how the Creator's son had died. All of a sudden, all the electricity went out at the Hopi Civic Center with the thousands of people attending. We thought that it was a part of the program. But, we found out later that the electricity had truly gone out at that precise moment when the ladies began wailing because Jesus had died. It was so silent that one could have heard a pin drop in that pitch dark auditorium and there was a holy hush.

Then, Rudy announced from the stage that the Son of the Creator (The Tribe had given specific instructions not to mention the name "Jesus") has risen! At that very moment, all the lights came back on as though someone had turned the light switch back on and the ladies began to give out shrills of high-pitched cries of victory. The men began to play their drums and joyful fast beats and the ladies went into a celebration Island dance which was so glorious and beautiful that it had awakened the whole crowd with rejoicing.

It was the Hopi Tribe who invited Island Breeze to come. We did not have to insist and do it our way or in our timing. It was God's timing for this nation to see how the Lord was working in other cultures to magnificently be glorified through the islanders. Al and Mima Brown, thank you for leading this amazing team!

Saguaro Cactus on our way up 87 from Phoenix to Flagstaff

Petroglyphs of migration symbols, and birds and animals and hands of the ancient ones are all over the southwest

Chapter 6

"Godliness and Contentment is a Great Gain"

Five more days until Christmas! I just read today that "Godliness with contentment is a great gain." (I Timothy 6:6). However, I realized I have not gained this great contentment here in Hopiland.

We have been without water in our home for three days because our main water pipe has been frozen in the ground out front. The village office is trying to take care of it today. I did not realize what it was like to not be able to flush the toilets, take showers, or wash the dishes like we used to. It is a good experience for us, since many Hopi live without running water all year long.

I also did not feel contentment when I fell flat on my back at the front door yesterday because of ice, nor when I had to clean out the ashes from the wood and coal-burning stove. Our house seems to cover itself with thin gray dust from the coal, like depression, and sometimes I just want to cry.

I do have contentment in other areas though, and we've come a long way since last Christmas. It was this exact time of the season last year that our daughter Naphtali took 16 pills because of loneliness. I do not believe it was her intention to kill herself but rather a desperate cry for help. We should have known better when we saw signs of depression such as her isolation, sleeping during the day and generally saddened mood. God has transformed her in mighty ways since that time.

The Scripture verse reminded me again that the Lord has called us here for a great assignment, and I can be really joyful even when cleaning up ashes. I must pick myself up and get ready for the 30 plus King's Kids, mostly under 18, who will arrive on December 26 to do their boot camp training. We are praying that the Hopi children will see this great example of young people using dance and drama to spread the Gospel.

Christmas in Hopiland

Christmas time in Hopiland was special. At the jail service, the inmates gave us one of the greatest Christmas gifts I've ever received. One of the Hopi inmates drew a Christmas bell, with many Hopi symbols. Many of the 60 male inmates had signed their greetings and names inside. They seemed very glad when I said, "Asquali," or "Thank You," in Hopi. When I said, "Owe," in response to something else, they all laughed because I had said it in First mesa accent. I should have said, "Owi," for "yes, you're welcome". The three mesas have each slightly different dialect. I was thankful that only seven women were in the jail during Christmas, which meant that all the rest were home with their families and children.

Because of funding from Compassion U.S.A., I was able to take 12 of the best Sunday school attendees to a movie, a park, and Burger King for dinner in Flagstaff the day after Christmas.

An 83-year old man invited me into his stone house for the first time when I went to pick up his teenage granddaughter to go with us. This old man (an elder in his village) with his traditional Hopi hair cut, held my hand while he sang the Beatles song to me "I Want To Hold Your Hand." We were both laughing and talked for awhile as he continued to hold my hand for a very long time.

A young boy, a child who is being trained to be a "Hopi Clown" (an honored position in the traditional Hopi dances and ceremonies), said as he was getting out of the van after our outing to Flagstaff, "Miss Millie, that was the funnest time I ever had." Miss Millie was how many Hopis addressed me, probably because I taught at the Mission School and Sunday School at Hotevilla Gospel church.

World Christian Indigenous Gathering

Will returned tonight after twelve days of attending the 2nd World Christian Gathering of Indigenous People in Rapid City, South Dakota.

Will wrote the following in an e-mail to our family and friends:

...The Lord's Spirit was there throughout the gathering, loving us through worship, praise, intercession, spiritual warfare, prophetic statements, teaching/preaching and more.

The gathering might have looked at first glance to be primarily about redeeming culture: art forms, music, language, dance, dress, customs, etc. but it was really about focusing on Jesus and what He is doing at this time with His Church and the unsaved world. This was of course mostly seen through the lens of the Spirit-filled indigenous people of the world.

Early on I helped pick up a large contingent of Maori people from

89

New Zealand. Sitting up front with me on the drive back from the airport were the 1996 founders of this Gathering, Monte and Linda Ohia. When Monte asked, I shared with him some of how God had directed us to Hopiland. One of the words to us had been that "The first shall be last and the last shall be first." He repeated that often during the conference. During the Praise March, while I was patrolling as the First Aid coordinator, Monte asked me to join him and the Maoris. They are a very warm people who know both the bitterness of being walked over by the Colonialists and the sweet joy of walking beside Jesus. They have a unique spiritual/cultural gift that God has and is redeeming, the Haka.

...God is doing something new (Is. 43:19), He is calling forth His children from the four directions (43:1-7). He is rousing Himself up like a warrior, raising a war cry. He will prevail against His enemies (42:13-17).

In times of intercession this war cry was raised up both with our voices and with Native drums redeemed for His glory and His purpose. The work done was not just the necessary ongoing reconciliation between Native and White, but the understanding that the Indigenous people have sinned also. Within animism, totemism and shamanism idols have been worshipped (44:9ff) and pacts have been made with death (28:14ff). There is an ongoing work of repentance and warfare, setting peoples free in these areas.

...What has kept most indigenous people out of the church is not Jesus but rather dead religion, legalism, judgementalism and narrow perspectives that seek to put our very big God in a little (often white man's) box...

When Millie and I were first seeking the Lord for direction a few years ago, He clearly told us that we were to go to the Hopi, to other tribes and to watch out for religious spirits. He did not say to watch out for Indians, or white people of Colonial backgrounds, or even rigid religious people. He said watch out for religious spirits. "For our struggle is not against flesh and blood but against the rulers, against the powers, against the world forces of this darkness, against the spiritual forces of wickedness in the heavenly places. Therefore, take up the full armor of God, that you may be able to resist in the evil day, and having done everything, to stand firm." — And having done everything, we will one day stand firm in the completed and fully realized victory of Jesus throughout the earth....

We drive 200 miles round-trip to downtown, Flagstaff to get one sewing machine needle among other things.
In this vast open space, one can see how the Israelites were led by the clouds during the Exodus days of Moses. One could easily see the contrasting shades on the ground, caused by the clouds in the sky, here in the desert.

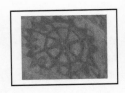

Chapter 7

The Bean Dance, The Crow Mother, The Ogre

All the villages will have their Bean Dance this weekend. The dance is a renewal, an invocation to the kachinas to intercede in behalf of the seeds that will soon be planted. The kachinas bring both blessings and warnings.

This is also a time when the children are initiated into the Kachina Society, the first of a long series of steps into spiritual adulthood. According to our Hopi friends, the kachinas bring both blessings and warnings.

We are told that the children will be whipped with yucca shoots by the kachinas and at one point, Crow Mother recites their youthful sins. During the whipping the godparent, who sponsors the child, will step in to protect the child and take the whipping themselves. It seems that this is symbolic of what Jesus had done for us. Yes, He has, indeed, taken the whipping for us. After three days of initiation, they will return home to have their hair ritually washed and receive a new Hopi name.

I have been curious about the Soyokos (ogres) who claim the bad children at this time. Apparently, a Soyoko Wuhti (ogre woman) with a red tongue hanging out between big fangs comes one day to warn that the ogres will arrive shortly. Soon after, there is a knock on the door. Along with a band of ogres, a huge and hideous woman who carries a basket strapped to her back, will ask for the bad child by name. The mother will have to beg for the child's pardon, and will offer flesh to appease the ogres. It is to bring shame and to humiliate the bad child in hope that repentance would bring a change into these misbehaving children. However, I am told by my Hopi friends that it does not really bring the change that is desired. This shaming method is so temporary that the children do not seem to take seriously what happens until next year.

Last night, during our Puhu Qatsi, ladies night, the women sounded so proud of their old traditional ways, but argued that the Soyokos are not effective because they only come once a year. The women all seemed weary from all the preparations of food and gifts, which are often obligatory pay-backs to keep others from getting upset. These gifts have lost the spirit of grace that was apparently once there in the old days. Today the people must keep records of the gift giving in order to manage the legalism that this has all evolved into.

The Ogres seem to represent an aspect of the Old Testament God to the Hopis. It would be easy to translate God as someone who is out to get people and to punish them when reading some parts of the Old Testament. But, I believe that it is never His intention to punish, but to love! One has to read ALL of the Sacred Word to know the true Nature and Character of God. I believe that if there had to be any violence against any human group, it was to destroy the plans of Satan, so that God can bring the Seed of the Messiah to us in order that He can reconcile us to Himself. He is good, kind and His mercy is everlasting to everlasting!

All Hopis are expected to participate in village dances, whether in dance, singing, cooking, baking, or to lend support by coming and eating. Their dances are said to be their way of praying (for rain, blessings, etc.). Out of our respect for Uberta Quimayosie, who has suffered much persecution for being a Christian and who has abstained from all participation in dances, we elected to support her by not attending at present. Someday, however, we sense that the time will come when we can attend some ceremonial and social dances, for we want to be with these people as Jesus lived among the Jews.

Black coal from the Peabody mine

We have been burning wood and chunks of black coal in our stove since the first of October. The coal which we get from the Peabody mine takes a two hour drive North of the Hopi reservation on the Navajo (Dine) reservation. Both the Hopi and Navajo lease land to Peabody Mine so all the residents on both of the reservations get two truck loads free every winter. We are thankful that the Hopi tribe is also giving us a coal card to be able to acquire coal. However, many are concerned and unhappy that Peabody mine is using millions of gallons of aquifer water out of the ground to sluice the coal.

One should get to the Peabody mine very early; otherwise, one ends up getting smaller coal chunks. The big ones are very black with smooth shiny pretty surfaces. It is a blessing to be able to use coal even though I do not like the smell, as it saves us so much on our propane bills. We would have to cut twice as much fire wood without using the coal. Just before going to sleep, all one needs is just one big size coal along with some wood in the stove to keep the house warm. In the morning, all the wood would be gone, but the coal would still be going with fiery red ember.

We have at least two more months before the cold season is over. And then, suddenly, with a little warmer weather, will come the highly erratic winds which will blow sand for the Spring months. And yet, what most visitors will call "inhospitable, harsh" desert land is where the ancient prophesies had directed these various Hopi clans to settle. They have vistas extending a hundred miles and with horizons interrupted by only mesas and buttes (small flat table top mountains).

We have still not stopped using our wood and coal stove for the house. It has been five months since we started heating our home. Some strong desert winds have started once again. I am thankful that it is still not so bad that I feel like a thousand sand flees have landed in my scalp as soon as I walk out of our home. I could still get to my van without having to close my eyes and feeling my way with my arms stretched out like a blind person.

Many responsibilities in the Hopi society

Once again, I saw the importance of Hopi dances during "Video night" at church. After slipping out of the room for tea and coming back, the children were getting up and dancing. Most Hopi are initiated into the Kachina Society, and later into men's and women's societies, and into priesthoods – the One Horn Society, Two Horn Society, and the Singers.

I have learned from Frank Waters book that many men, by choice, do not enter these priesthoods, nor, in fact, are allowed to enter the One Horn, Two Horn, and the singer society. The priesthood carries with it awesome and secret responsibilities for the religious affairs of the Hopi. Each society has special knowledge and wisdom, unknown even to the other societies. We have been told that the One Horn Society has the responsibility of giving a newly appointed Bear Clan leader (the Priesthood Clan) the authority to carry out the duties of his office, and that the One Horns are the enforcers, often with rather grim duties, such as eliminating intruders into the initiation rites. The Two Horns are philosophers, and the Singers consecrate decisions that are made. The truly deep

Hopi religion lies in these societies.

Hotevilla no longer has Soyoko woman and ogres coming to their village due to the death of several children some decades back. One child, who was being grabbed by the ogres behind his mother, became so terrified that he began having nightmares and then died. Two other children died soon after. The village people went to the Chief and begged him not to allow the Soyoko and ogres to return, and, since he had grandchildren of his own and didn't want this to happen to them, he agreed.

When I went to pick up a friend up at Hotevilla village, she came out of her house and asked me to drive away quickly. This is because the kachinas had come out of the eight kivas in that village and were roaming around and whipping any cars with the head lights on. We could not have our ladies' fellowship at the home of one of our ladies for she had too much she owed to her relatives, and had to work to pay back.

On February 22, I was invited to come over and eat with one of the families. They served me Bean sprout soup, the traditional soup with sprouts which were grown by the Kachinas in various kivas and brought to the family. Before eating, the head of the family sprinkles cornmeal outside the door to honor the Kachina spirits. However, when we were ready to eat, they asked me to pray for the meal.

120 Native American drums

We found out that Linda Prince, a native Christian from Canada went to Israel and entered the Knesset, the Jewish Parliament, wearing her regalia, as the Lord had commanded her. What a surprise it must have been when the Jewish religious leaders came and bowed to the floor and worshipped God, saying that she was of the "Lost Tribe." They also asked why she had not brought the "Warriors." So the Lord gave her a vision to have 120 hand drums made to take back to Israel and to be played by Native American warriors. Will was privileged to join them when the 120 drums were dedicated at YWAM Richardson Springs, near Chico, California, to our God and His Son, Jesus.

Our lives in Hopiland

I felt desperately lonely the other night as I drove the last 100 mile stretch of the desert, coming back from California. It is hard here. I felt as though I might as well have been in Timbuktu, Africa. But, I was driving back the 15 passenger van which YWAM Salem, Oregon had donated and I was so grateful! I no longer have to have 12-17 kids in my 5 passenger Caravan for our Sunday video nights. That was like trying to stuff as many people into a telephone booth. God is so good!

Sometimes, I don't know how to rest or where to go in this land. It is not like we can go out alone to a coffee shop when we need to unwind and talk for there is only one restaurant in Second Mesa, the Hopi Cultural Center, and one will see practically every other Hopi and all the tourists there. I sense such a weight of the heaviness from all the ceremonies and dances out here every weekend for the last couple of months.

Bacavi Youth Center desires to build a big 'ropes course." They have taken 5 trips with Will and want him to be able to build the course at the Hopi Civic Center location. How great it would be to have this tool available as an alternative to drugs and alcohol.

A woman from Hotevilla came by to ask if I could buy some pottery that her mother had made in 1984. This mother of three of my Sunday School children needed to sell this simple but elegant "Piki Bowl" in order to pay for her son's glasses. The bowl had no designs painted on it but it was handmade and baked outside the traditional way, with sheep dung. She was asking only $150 but I knew it was worth so much more because her mother, Violet Huma, from the village of Sichmovi, had been a potter and Violet's work is displayed at the Museum of Northern Arizona.

The "Luke Film" is being translated into the Hopi language. The project has been put on hold until some Hopi men will volunteer to read the men's part. Jim MacCormack has undertaken this project with a couple of Hopi Christian ladies.

There are now four, later five students at the YWAM Native Christian Boot Camp, four natives and one Pahana. Daniel and Heleen have proceeded in great faith to see the school get started. They didn't have any students at all on the first day and Heleen cried as we sat around the table and ate by ourselves. As they prayed the students started arriving.

Pulling down of a mask

During a dance in March, someone ran up and pulled down a mask from a Kachina in Second Mesa. This could have a devastating effect on some children, since they are believed to be the spirits that bring rain. We did not find out why this one Hopi person went up and unmasked this one kachina.

Grim Statistics

By 1900, only 237,000 Natives survived the diseases, wars and relocations. The fetal Alcohol syndrome is 33 times higher amongst the Native Americans than the non-Natives. And one in six native adolescents has attempted suicide, a rate four times higher than that of non-Natives. In 1997, 75% of Natives earned less than $7,000. We have an unreached nation right here in the United States

Our God is a covenant keeper. Israel went through three years of famine because King Saul broke one 400 year old covenant with a local tribe called the Gibeonites. There are over 400 treaties broken by the U.S. government with the tribes of North America.

An elderly Hopi woman; afraid to die

A mother of three of my Sunday School kids came to visit me this March day. As a licensed elderly care person, she was visiting a lady in the village of Polacca. While there, the elderly woman had an "out of body" experience, of going down to the Grand Canyon. The place from which the Hopi believe they emerged into this Fourth World is an opening in the ground called the "Sipapu" down in the canyon. The Creator had judged the world three times prior because of human wickedness. They also believe they will go back to the Grand Canyon when they die.

The elderly lady said she saw many who were walking around in Hopi clothes, and saw those whom she knew had gone before her. She told my friend that she was frightened to go back to this place. My friend, then, became frightened because this woman should not be afraid of going to the Hopis traditional place of death, especially since she had heard that this Hopi paradise would be such a beautiful place to go.

This mother said that she had also been visiting another lady in Kykotsmovi and this lady had been hearing the sound of an owl hooting very loudly at night. This woman was not frightened about this owl because she is a Christian. However, her family was petrified that she will die because the owl is believed to be a "messenger of death."

The men and the boys have been in the kivas in Hotevilla for three days, and there will be dances again this weekend, and another dance in Shongopovi also simultaneously.

What about the academics?

We were invited with Clover and Naphtali to attend the First Hopi High Academic Awards Banquet. After attending the Sports Awards Banquet last year, I felt it was important that Hopi High also awarded those in good Academic standing, so that basketball and track is not the only thing that is glorified for the Hopi youth. I talked to a couple of teachers, Tom Mentzor and David Loveland and they took this to the School Board and made the yearly Academic Awards Banquet happen. Thank you Mr. Mentzor and Mr. Loveland and the School Board of Hopi High School!

An office in our garage

Craig & Geri Colgrove, Sheila Meadows, and the other members of Word of Grace church in Mesa, Arizona came to build an office in our garage and to build an attic for storage of Will's Sea and Summit equipment. I could not believe how different our garage looked only after a weekend of work. No more overhead projector and boxes of Bibles for the Jail ministry in our bedroom, no more Art supplies and Sunday school materials in our room, and no more Women's ministry supplies also in our closet. Yeah, thank you Lord!

A Hopi wedding

In May there was a big wedding in Hotevilla, and everyone was busy preparing for it. Jane Sekayumptewa showed me over 350 sacks of flour to be given away to the groom's side of the family. There were over 40 pies and many cakes, with boxes and boxes of piki bread, the blue cornmeal traditional Hopi paper thin bread, along with many trash cans full of ground corn.

The bride goes to the groom's house to grind corn for three days to prove that she is a strong and steady worker who is worthy of marriage. Saturday I am invited to the wedding and will eat with the family. On Tuesday, I have been invited to go up to their house before sunrise to watch the bride come home in her all-white outfit and moccasins which her uncle made.

The men on the groom's side kill a few sheep and a cow, the ladies drain the blood to mix with blue corn meal, and then it is put back into the sheep's stomach lining to be baked in the ground. The "blood cake" will be eaten at the wedding.

Once, we were invited to come and see the bride's family and her clan, come to bring gifts to the groom's family. It was like a long parade of cars which came into the village where the groom's family lives. People came out of their cars and began to bring the boxes and plastic laundry baskets full of food. It seemed like an endless line of food which was taken into a small stone house only to be taken out the back door by a long line of the groom's family after there was no more room left in the house.

It seems that there has been more of a competition amongst the families to outdo the others in recent past. It used to be very humble in the past especially when the food used to be scarce. Now, everything is recorded in a book to someday pay back all that was brought. The more one gives, the more one is expected to get back someday when their sons and daughters get married. We were sharing in our Puhu Qatsi, (New Life) ladies' group that this pay back system needs to be done differently. Too often, it has become a show rather than giving out of love and generosity. The sad thing is that this engaged couple did not stay together in the end.

As the ladies talked about this, they were realizing that it may need to start with them to give out of humility and sincerity rather than to show off how rich one may be. However, when someone is well off and can give generously, to welcome the bride or the groom into the family by extravagantly giving, one could hardly find fault in this. It is only when the ones who are not as well off, are expected to pay back.

Chapter 8

Only One Peach Tree and Christmas in Hopi

Sometimes, it is hard to look through rose-colored glasses. Ministering in Hopiland is hard and feels hopeless at times, like tending my garden. One peach tree has died during this cold winter and another peach tree, despite my tender loving care, now seems to be dying as well. Only one out of four fruit trees is thriving. Harsh sandy soil, lacking in fertile nutrients, and the wind blowing mercilessly and threshing the delicate flowers causes growing attempts to be difficult.

> *Lord, all my desire is before you,*
> *and my sighing is not hidden from you.*
> *(Psalms 38:9)*

Disappointments and discouragements have overtaken me. The dances have started again and there are only five little ones to ride in the newly purchased 15-passenger van. Sometimes, I am on the verge of breaking out and crying throughout the day when no one is around. One of the two Hopi ladies who signed up for YWAM Christian Native School has dropped out.

The Eagles for Sacrifice

A bald eagle on Leupp Road, near our house in Flagstaff

By August most of the eagles and hawks are gone from Hotevilla. There were approximately 20 on top of the roofs of different homes (some having 3 or 4 eagles). These eagles have an enormous wing span. They were chained up and fed daily. They were sacrificed on August 1, and such a heavy spirit was over the village. While dropping off the children from Sunday School, two men were in the process of sacrificing a squawking hawk. Eagles are smothered so that no blood will be shed.

A Great fear in the village

There was great fear in the village of Shungopovi last weekend, according to a Hopi friend, because the Antelope priests were walking around. No one dares to come out of their houses for fear they will die. This is a very serious matter. The mesas are shrouded in cold and dark mysteries that no one dares challenge.

103

Baby naming and hair washing

Last week, before the sunrise, we were able to visit a Hopi Christian couple's home. They were hosting a baby-naming ceremony for their granddaughter's baby. This was the 21st day after the birth. The baby's hair was first washed, with water and a yucca plant, by the aunt, and then all the other relatives went up afterwards to wash and stroke the baby's hair gently with a perfect ear of corn. A believing Hopi friend tells us that the perfect ear of corn represents the perfect life, which can only point to Jesus.

All the relatives presented their gifts to the baby's mother, wrapping her with layers of beautiful blankets. The baby was also given many blankets and gifts, and each relative presented the baby a name such as "itsy, bitsy spider" (because she was from the spider clan), among other names.

The baby, at last, was taken outside to meet Dawa, the sun, for the first time, and prayers were offered by two aunts. Although it had been Hopi custom to offer cornmeal to the spirits, it was not done this time. Then everyone was asked to sit down and was served corn pudding that had been cooking all night in the ground. What a feast!

Established in the old NPC building

In order to get our electricity, telephone, water, and gas turned on in the old NPC (Northland Pioneer College) building which we are renting, Will had to go to the governor's office in our village of Kykotsmovi. He had to get a business license from the Hopi Tribal office and, even though they knew we were in Christian ministry, they approved it. This is the first time we have come out and publicly acknowledged that were are with YWAM International Ministries. Prior to this we felt it would be best to not advertise ourselves in any way, but take time to build trust relations. We have chosen not to put any ministry signs in front of the building.

A Christmas parade and lights in Hopiland

Christmas lights are lit up all over Hopiland. There were so few lights a few years ago that I felt out of place as I hung the lights, and yet, I wanted to light up our place as Jesus said the He is the light of the world. There are now lights galore in the Hopi Tribal Housing area, all along the highways, and in different villages. I would like to believe that this is a representation of God's light shining on the Hopi people.

Also, for the first time in the village of Hotevilla, they have decided to have a Christmas parade on Christmas Eve. It felt as though the village might have scheduled this event at the same time as our Church Christmas program. The village is having three Hopi kachinas to come and dance in the plaza to open the underground kivas for next year. Some Hopi say that these Kachinas are like the "three wise men" but they are also called "Pharisees." After this parade, everyone is invited to the Hotevilla Community Center where Santas will hand out presents to all the children. However, the children must be present to receive the gifts. Uberta said that this was the first time the village has tried to interfere with the Christmas programs at the Church.

The ambulance and police cars were decorated with lights for the village parade and were blocking the road near the Church. Recognizing my car, they allowed me to go through the barricade. Our Christmas program started with the ladies singing the Christmas Carols. There were not that many people that night and no children as they were all over at the big event at the Hotevilla Community Center. The children had practiced for so many weeks to be in our Christmas pageant and I was pacing in the back of the Church wondering and praying as to what I needed to do. Do I just sit and do nothing or do I go to the Community Center and ask for the children.

I felt that the Lord wanted me to go to the Community Center where three Santas were in the front. One Hopi lady, seeing me, signaled me to go up to the announcer and ask. The place was so packed out that I was barely able to get to the front. So, I made an announcement that all the children scheduled to be in our Christmas

Navajo sandstone Nativity figurines
We are encouraging the Hopi believers to
make Hopi nativity carvings

play needed to come at once. All but one child came with me as they were promised that the presents would be saved for them. It was a beautiful play!

A few days later, we were asked to come and sing at the Hopi Civic Center for their "Toys for Tots" Christmas event. About 30 of us, the women from Hotevilla, our Thursday evening ladies' group, and Hotevilla Sunday School kids got up and sang in front of about 1,000 Hopi people. We welcomed the Holy Spirit's presence to come and to give the King of kings the glory He deserves without the Hopi people even knowing.

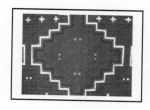

Chapter 9

The Bean Sprouts Raised in the Kiva

The Bean Dance was held this past weekend up at Hotevilla. The bean sprouts are raised down in the kivas and everyone is invited to come and eat at various homes. The men have already been down in their kivas preparing themselves for days for the dance. I was so surprised that the children still wanted to go down to Phoenix with me as our Sunday School trip had already been planned. Even as I was picking up the children early Saturday morning, the village was alive with excitement.

Three kachinas were walking right behind our van and I thought one was coming over to chase me away. However, he came and gave a gift, a mud head doll, to a child standing by the road. He was half naked with a mask and bells and feathers around his ankles and wrists. A couple of nights ago, as I was going around visiting the children, I was warned by one of the kids to be careful because the kachinas were walking around outside.

The night before, the Soyoko had already come out several times from the kiva and brought gifts to the children. The legend has it that long ago, when her mother was braiding her hair and only one side of her hair was braided, the enemy force came into the village and she was able to run out and defeat all the enemy warriors. Depicted by a man with a mask, she then became the mother of all kachinas.

The Buffalo Dance

The Buffalo Dance was held in my village of Kykotsmovi. One of the ladies in my Puhu Qatsi group could not come to the meeting because her son was chosen by a girl to dance. Gifts such as cakes and bread which were made at home by the mother needed to be taken to her family. A shawl which the young man was able to buy himself, out of what he earned from his carvings, will be taken to the girl's house.

A Valentines surprise; airplane ride

The Hopi children and I had a Valentine's treat we will never forget. Three retired pilots in Phoenix gave us airplane rides. Some children were in the air for almost an hour, perhaps something that they, nor any of their friends, will ever experience again. We were so thankful to the Begleys and other friends at Word of Grace.

The New Student Body President at Hopi High

Our 17-year old daughter, Naphtali, has been voted Student Body President of Hopi High School. When she first told me that she was going to run for this office against a Hopi girl who was an honor student, I did not know how to respond. There is a very tight social fabric in Hopi society between the clans and all the relatives. I did not want to see her disappointed if she did not win, and I figured that I would just have to mop up after her once this is done. And yet I realized she had already won, no matter what, for she dared to do what she believed she needed to do. It was a very close race, but she won by 20 votes, it showed us the tremendous favor our daughter had at Hopi High School amongst her peers. She may be the very first Christian Student Body President at Hopi High School, and perhaps the first non-Hopi to be elected.

A Mother-Daughter Tea Party

On Mother's Day, our YWAM facility in Kykotsmovi was opened to host a "Mother-Daughter Tea Banquet." It was much fun to have all the tea cup sets and the flowery tea pots with all the different types of tea to serve all the mothers and the daughters. Also the girls from the Girl's Club read their poems.

Millie's tea pots and tea cups

Tae-kwon-Do classes in Hopiland

A Korean pastor had come out a couple of years ago, and started some Tae-kwon-do classes. Even after he had stopped coming, some others carried on his work. 15 Hopi students have been accepted to enter Jr. Tae-kwon-do Championship in July in Texas, but they have now lost their teacher/master and the parents are heartbroken.

The Korean Martial Arts has been very successful here in Hopiland with the little ones, and the parents and the teachers have noticed more respect and discipline in these kids' lives. Last year, some of the Hopi children were able to attend a Championship event in Seoul, Korea and came back speaking a little bit of Korean. They are asking for another Tae-kwon-do master to come and help teach the children.

The Korean dancers in Walpi

The Hopi people were very surprised when they found out our Korean team was invited to Walpi village, on top of First Mesa, especially when the Flute Dance preparation was being done in the kivas up there by the men. Our last Korean group from California did their beautiful traditional fan dance at the "Ponsi Hall" on top of one of the most unique mesa villages that one would ever see in the world.

The cliff sides are perhaps three hundred feet or more and the mesa narrows to only ten feet before entering the village. This wonderful team charmed the people up there with their singing and choreographed hand and body motions, and Tae-kwon-do. Ponsi Hall was once a church many years ago but was eventually abandoned. It is now the office that visitors go to for the Walpi Village guided tours. This is one of the Hopi villages that claim to be the oldest. It is the only guided tour in all of Hopi.

I was exhausted by the time this Korean group left. And what a sweet witness they were to this community of God's wonderful love, especially on Friday night at the Hopi Mission School when about 150 Hopi people showed up, and so many of them were young teens and families. Thank you, Global Mission Church! Glory to God!!

We thank also the Korean group from "Light of Love Church" who came the first nine days of August, bringing in Hip-Hop Dance for the young teens, and Korean jacks, and a Martial Arts team, and so much more at the Civic Center. We got good reports about them doing the jail ministries and Vacation Bible School in Hotevilla while we were on vacation. Thanks to our special friend Eddie Song!

Hopi leaders in our facility

It was an honor when our Hopi Tribal Vice-Chairman showed up at our YWAM building and stretched his hand out saying, "I just came by to say thanks for all the work you are doing here and for our community." Then another morning this week, a very important Hopi man (reminds me of Nicodemus), showed up in our living room and said, "I need to talk to someone. I lost my wife and family through alcoholism, and I have been sober almost a year, but things have been very tough and I need help. Can I talk to you guys?" I am in awe of how God is working.

Wukoki ruins near Flagstaff, Arizona
800 years ago, some Hopi clans lived here.

111

Chapter 10

A Symphony in Australia!

We were invited by Mua and Marie Vae from YWAM Victoria, BC, Canada to join a First Nations outreach to New Zealand and the Sydney Olympics. Mua is Samoan and Marie is native. Will went ahead of me to join the team in Canada. He went with them on the first leg of the outreach to the Hui, or gathering, for the inauguration of YWAM's new international president, Frank Naea. Frank is Samoan and Maori. Apparently it was an amazing, colorful and beautiful event. Will said that at the conclusion he had been invited to join a group of twenty Maori and other island elders who debriefed the gathering. He was so proud of YWAM that they let them do the Hui their own way, island style. It was our introduction to God's call to the Pacific Rim indigenous peoples.

Being on the Sydney Olympics Outreach was not always easy, but it was very good! Often, we went early morning to late night, riding the rails into Sydney doing train evangelism, or doing open-air dramas, songs and testimonies, and working with churches. One week, we were able to be in the worst ghetto area called "the Block" near Sydney where syringes lay everywhere on the ground from the heroin addicts blatantly shooting up around us. And yet, we saw God's hope there and we believe that we will be going back there some day with the Hopi believers. We did see one Olympic event; wrestling was the only event that was not sold out and was somewhat affordable on our "free" day.

One thing I had desired to do so desperately while in Australia was to attend a symphony at the Sydney Opera House. Every day, I would go by the Event posters and longingly look at the

*Sydney Opera House in
Darling Harbor in Australia*

various groups who would perform. I had suggested to Will that we go and see at least one event and he had clearly told me that our finances would not allow it. Then, came the Opening night of the Olympics! It was reported that there were an estimated 22,000 people in the Darling Harbor area. This would have been my last chance to attend a symphony there and once again, Will had said "No." I could have insisted and most likely gotten my way and yet, I sensed in my spirit that I was to decline to Will without giving him an argument. I felt sad, nevertheless, as I felt that we were being herded like the cows in an arena as we were walking in the harbor, away from the Sydney Opera House.

Suddenly, I felt a tap on my shoulder from behind me. This one lady stopped me in the middle of some 22,000 people or more walking around the Darling Harbor area. She lifted two tickets in her hand, and asked me, "Would you like these two tickets to the symphony tonight?" I was so shocked that I could hardly speak. She continued and said, "My daughter is too tired to stay."

It was an amazing picture of My Father's love for me. What a wonderful display of His sweet kindness. He who knew the desire of His daughter's heart and so lavishly provided! When He saw that the little girl got tired inside the Opera House, He had them get up out of their seats just at the precise second to come out to the Darling Harbor, to get right behind me in that huge throng of people that night, and then rather than just tossing the tickets in the trash after they got home, had the mother ask me whether I wanted those two tickets to the symphony!

The New Zealand Symphony played that evening, and the Maori queen was ushered onto the stage by Sir Edmund Hilary who was the first to climb Mt. Everest. What an incredible treat it was for Will and I to see his South Pole Expedition on the giant screen, as Sir Edmund was reading his book, and the symphony was playing all at the same time!

Men's Talking Circle at Hopi Jail and other ministries

Two new things that are going on in Hopiland are, after doing jail ministry for over three years, it has been opened up to do another night to be able to do "A Talking Circle" for those inmates who are more serious about being discipled. This is a miracle because we have tried many times to get this extra night and it was not allowed before. When some Hopi inmates started asking for it, Daniel and Terry, on our Tribal Winds team, began going in to meet with a smaller group of men for a modified form of Talking Circle. A talking circle normally in Indian country is a circle of people who respectfully take turns speaking about what is on their hearts. Our talking circles evolved with our different leaders. This one consists of worship, sometimes a short Bible study, talking circle and prayer.

It was so nice to have Terry and Darlene Wildman leading worship, with guitar and a Jim-be drum from Madagascar, at the Hopi Jail church service last night for the men. The Wildmans joined us this year following an unusual chain of God led events. We had met them last year at the home of a Navajo friend, James Skeet, in Phoenix. Terry and James were leading us all in wonderfully anointed worship when the Spirit fell.

Will started laughing in the Spirit; he had never done this before. When he finally stopped, we asked him what that was about. Will said, God had told him, "It is not about us!" He said that he couldn't stop laughing for he was so relieved. This message went deep into the core of his being this time, deeper than he had ever understood before. Our life and work is not about us but it is about the Lord God Himself.

Next, he came over to Terry and "commissioned" him and Darlene for native ministry. He then continued to surprise us by telling Terry that the Lord said he should grow his hair long. We now know that Terry has some Yaqui Indian blood but what was God doing? The Lord next, within a couple weeks, told the Wildman's through their pastor to go right away to a YWAM DTS. They did that last year and then came out to join us here in Hopi.

After being refreshed from coming back from Australia, Will and I were able to go into jail ministry on Monday. There were about forty men who came in, and I was so in love with Jesus that I did not even mind when Will talked to the men with his reading glasses hanging down off his nose. (Now, I read with my reading glasses down on my nose too) We showed our slide show from New Zealand and Australia and told them how God's people were worshipping the Lord within their own culture. We told them how God had given us many wonderful contacts with the Aborigine Christians in Australia and how they are very anxious for the Native American believers to come to their land to tell their stories. We also had time with the ladies afterwards and then the juvenile boys at the third service. I believe that this is a new concept to many of them, not to have to cut their hair and dress or sing as white men, or even to be allowed to dance as a Christian (King David certainly did).

On another occasion two of the Hopi ladies in our "New Life" group and I led the service for the women. As we start to see Hopi believers coming in to share Jesus with other Hopis we are seeing fulfillment of our vision for an indigenous expression of Hopi church.

The Lord spares our daughter

Clover's country window by her crib which I painted for her when she was a baby
The road leads to a yellow house.
Along the way are many flowers.

I would like to tell you of God's goodness in my family's lives. Our first daughter, Clover, was in a car accident recently. (No, that is not the good news). The other driver ran a red light, hitting our car hard enough to have our Grand Caravan declared "totaled." Clover walked away from the accident with minor aches and bruises from the air bag which opened up. What we believe as God's goodness is that her little tiny Toyota would not turn over when she got in to start it up that morning. So, she had to take our Caravan to the university. How thankful we are that our Lord knew what was coming and stopped her little car, which was without the air bag. We know that she was safe, because of God's kindness towards us. She only had some bruises on her arms

Naphtali's First Request at Hopi High

As a new Student Body President at Hopi High, our daughter, Naphtali's first meeting with faculty did not go that well. She felt that her first assignment was to ask whether she could have a weekly Bible study and prayer in one of the classrooms during a lunch hour. The faculty, perhaps not knowing quite how to respond, recommended that she have another meeting with the Principal. Naphtali met with the principle and was told, "No," for this is Hopiland. (After all, they have their own religion.) This was challenged by another teacher, Mr. Wirth, who said that when it is student initiated that she is allowed to do this. The Principal came to Naphtali later and announced that the group can meet to have a Bible study and prayer at Hopi High.

There were eight other kids who showed up to join together for a Bible study with Naphtali and John this week. In the history of that high school, this KFC, "Kids For Christ," group would be the first to honor Jesus. We thank God for the girl's softball coach who is a Christian, who has sponsored them and made it possible for them to use the room.

It would be hard to explain to anyone the miracle of having Hopi and Navajo kids show up for Bible studies on the Hopi High School campus. One must realize that to be associated with any Christian activities is very much ostracized in this very strong ceremonial land. And yet these high school kids are showing up for the Bible study and to pray, during their lunch hour once a week. On average, 8 to 12 are gathering every Wednesday.

A Baptism and a wedding

There has been another baptism this past week. Yes, only the second since we have come to Hopiland. The Lord touched this woman's life while she was in jail over a year ago, and her partner also received Jesus while he was serving another sentence. Now, they also decided to marry after many years of being together and having several children. They wanted to make things right with God. It was a beautiful wedding with Hopi outfits, which her mom made for all those in the wedding party. There was even a traditional mud fight afterwards between the two families outside.

The Fall Festival

One of the ladies in our New Life group asked whether we can have an alternative event at the YWAM facility on Halloween night. She said she no longer wanted her children involved in what originated as a Satanic activity and we needed to let her people also know. So we will have a "Fall Festival" on the 31st. It is our hope that we would be able to have hay rides, fun booths, craft tables and other activities outside all around the building for the children. We have been discussing an outreach to Australia next year with the Puhu Qatsi ladies, so we will do our first fundraiser for the airfares by making and selling Hopi Tacos at this event.

The Fall Festival, which was held at the YWAM facility, was a huge success. We believe it was the Lord who brought more than 200 people to this event. There were many volunteers from the community who manned different booths such as "Donuts on a String," clown toss, craft tables, Hopi Taco sale and the Ropes Course events outside, along with some other games which were going non-stop all evening. We were glad that this was initiated by a Hopi Christian. Those who came with the scary costumes were politely asked to take them off and we were able to set a precedent for the future years to say that god is love, not of fear, and that we do not want little children getting scared at this event.

118

Evaluating Short term summer teams

We, as YWAM Northern Arizona, are praying and re-evaluating where we are with our visions and goals about being in Hopiland. We especially have to look at the short-term mission teams coming in to help with VBS and other works. We don't want to perpetuate dependence on missionaries and we don't want to make the same mistakes by doing the same old mission things that have been going on out here for the past 100 years. Even though it seems almost impossible for these handfuls of Hopi Christians to do all the programs themselves, how many teams do we allow in order to bring the good news of Jesus?

So do we never bring any groups in because this should be the responsibility of the Hopi Christians? And if we don't have any programs all summer long when the children are totally bored, what then? Is it worth bringing in Christian youth to mingle with the Hopi youth and rub shoulders together, and is it worth bringing them in so that at least the Hopi youth who never would come to church otherwise can hear the Gospel? And yet, how long do we do this before the Hopi church becomes self-perpetuating and growing on their own? If the Lord wants us to totally lay down hosting any more groups, I want to be willing. We as a team are waiting and praying about this radical point.

December in Hopiland

The winter is a quiet time here in Hopiland for the people. Many of the men go down to the kivas to meditate and pray. Would you pray with us during this time that the Lord would speak to those who are seeking Him earnestly? We see so many people coming to know the Lord in their hearts, but we don't really see the Sunday morning services growing that much at all. Perhaps, God has another plan to see His church out here in Hopiland develop and grow like the ones that met in various home churches as in the New Testament days. We imagine that many of these believers are like

119

the plants in the Hopi fields. The seeds have germinated but the shoots are hiding below the surface waiting for a time of safety and more watering before they stick their heads above the surface. It is very scary to be labeled Ka Hopi, Not Hopi, by your family and friends.

Yet another Hopi person died this past week. It was Loretta's mom. Loretta is the one who had received the Lord in jail awhile back and was baptized with her son this year. For almost three years, her mother would not hear of Loretta speaking of Jesus. But only two weeks before she died, she could not reject the love of Christ and the evidence of God's work in her daughter's life. When the coffin was delivered to the home to be mourned over, songs of praise rang throughout that home. The traditional relatives had their way to mourn all night and to bury her body in the morning, but we know she is dancing with our Lord!

Uberta told the ladies up at our Hotevilla Gospel Church that they need to be an indigenous church and be able to provide for the materials needed on their own. So the ladies cooked all day to make tamales and "somiviki" (Hopi blue cornmeal wrapped in corn husks), and had a sale. Now they have enough money to be able to buy wood to heat the church and get coal for the Winter season.

Sunday School kids down in Phoenix

I am leaving this morning for Phoenix, 4 hours from Hopiland, with 12 children to go skating, to an amusement park, to the YMCA to go swimming and to see a Christmas play at Word of Grace Church this weekend. We will practice Hopi Christmas songs so they can sing at the church Christmas program even though I won't be there. I really want to be with my family this Christmas in California. My eighty four year old friend, Ida Walking Bear, will be going down with us too. She is one of my best and dearest friends here.

Hotevilla Gospel Church has purchased the 1985 Ford 15-passenger van with $9,000 down and $175 monthly payments for 3 years.

*Our little Hopi friends dancing around
the fire in our back yard*

*A Kiva ladder going up to the entrance door of the roof
at Spruce Tree House in Mesa Verde, Colorado*

Chapter 11

Not Enough Feathers to Give Out

According to one of my ladies in Puhu Qatsi, there were only five old Hopi men who went down to purify themselves in the kiva in her village, to pray for the blessings for the world in December. These five men did not have enough Eagle feathers to give out to all the residents of Hotevilla, as a blessing, as is traditional, so they only went to their immediate families. The Hopis have an ancient prophecy that their religion will some day die and that "Pahana," their long awaited True Brother, will come to show them the way to the Father Above. Like the Jews, they are still waiting for this Messiah, the "Pahana" when Jesus has already come! We the Church are privileged to be able to Re-present Him as true brothers and sisters ourselves.

Afraid to be in my own home

I was realizing that I lived in fear all day when Will and all our kids were gone on New Year's Day. I was afraid to even make a fire in our wood stove for the fear that the smoke would be seen and that a neighbor may come over. I was even afraid to answer the phone or open my door. We had received a call after midnight on New Year's morning from this young man whom we have been involved with now for four years. He is such a beautiful young man with such a gift of poetry and songs and there is an incredible potential for him to be anything he wants to be. However, when he is in a drunken state, he can be very unpredictable and not trustworthy. Now, I know how it feels to be scared in ones own home. But then the Lord gave me His wonderful confidence that our safety was, indeed, in His hands. Our God calls this young man "a child of God" and showed me that "I want what I want, when I want" which was that I wanted this young man to grow up right NOW. I am not afraid anymore.

Native facilitators

We are hosting a "YWAM Native Ministries Conference" in January, 2001. Our small YWAM facility in Kykotsmovi will be overflowing with Native facilitators, local people and YWAMers from the U.S. and Canada. We will fellowship and discuss what the future Native church would look like in Hopiland and elsewhere when the longed for revival breaks out.

I had so much anxiety coming into this conference, but felt at the same time that God might just have something really special for us. In the midst of major winter storming that kept at least a half dozen people away we had an amazing time together with the Lord and each other.

22 years together

After our Conference, Will and I drove 100 miles in a snowstorm near the Flagstaff area to get down to Phoenix. We had received a free 2-night package deal to Catalina Island almost a year ago by sitting through a sales pitch. We thought we would use it for our belated twentieth wedding anniversary. We thought there must be a catch as to why they were giving away this package for this certain time, but the weather conditions and our two nights in Catalina turned out to be very special!

Twenty-two years together (In Winslow- 50 miles East of Flagstaff) 2002

It was 22 years ago in 1979 when I was engaged to Will and moved into what was called the "Winterhouse," which originally was a group home for those lost kids, wards of the court, who did not have a home after our summer mountain program. This place was a part of "Sea & Summit Expedition's" ministry in downtown Santa Barbara.

When Will and I got married and became the Sea & Summit Directors, we had an expanded vision. God led us into working with Christian young adults who the Church in Santa Barbara did not know how to help. I was to start the Girls' Discipleship Apartment downstairs.

A ripped wedding gown

Before our wedding, my first roommate, at the discipleship house, was a run away 13-year old girl whose mother was in prison. I didn't know what I would be missing every day when I came back from work; even my underwear drawer was no longer mine. I never forgot one day, I had an urgent sense to look in my closet.

To my horror, she had gone through and tried on all my dresses, and had not even bothered to hang some of my dresses back on the hanger. And then, I was stunned to find that she had taken out my wedding gown tucked far away in the back of the closet, which was to be worn only on that very special day. It was a very simple gown that my friend Claire helped me pick out on State Street in Santa Barbara. This girl was a bit bigger than I, therefore, a part of my dress was ripped, and I was so sad. I was able to fix it and still wear it, and it was so beautiful.

To connect more to the Hopi world

Since resigning at Hopi Mission School as their Art teacher for Kindergarten through Sixth grade, and working at their library, I've desired more to connect with the real Hopi world. I have been asked to teach Art at the schools of Hotevilla/ Bacavi School and at the Hopi Day School in Kykotsmovi. Will and I have been both asked to be on the Board of Directors for the Hopi Day School, and the Hopi Vice-Chairman's office just called asking whether I would like to be on their Fourth of July Celebration Committee. How faithful our Lord has been to give us so much favor and now I need to choose how to serve our God best.

After having worked with the school and the church for four and a half years, I believe that the Lord is now calling me to do more home visits. I am always surprised how so many people in Hotevilla greet me by saying, "Oh, hi Miss Millie. It's you," when I don't even know who they are. I believe God simply wants me to go to homes and sit and listen and ask whether they have any prayer requests.

Seven tickets to Australia

We have now purchased tickets for our team of 7 people to go to Australia. What an amazing thing it is now to be able to take several of our Native American friends to a distant land as missionaries.

As I have said previously, Loretta accepted the Lord in Hopi Jail. She grew up in First Mesa, below the village of Walpi. She got baptized with her 15-year old son, Albert, last year. Her mother passed away recently and Loretta is still going through a grieving stage. Loretta has been teaching and sharing her testimonies on Bible study nights at the "Hope Cottage" Women's Shelter in Flagstaff, where she also got help once. Since making the decision to go on the Australia Outreach, the enemy had come full force to bring her down, e.g., two different accidents at work.

Debbie grew up all her life in Kykotsmovi in Hopiland. She has been a part of our weekly "Puhu Qatsi" (New Life) ladies' fellowship, and is growing so fast we could hardly keep up.

Pastor Ken oversees 15 churches in Navajo land, and has started many other churches. He is anointed to pray for people and is gentle in the way he conducts ministries. He is already looking forward to taking his wife and his 30-year old son (who is also quite a man of God) to go on future outreaches with us.

Gerri grew up in the village of Hotevilla and has a real desire to serve the Lord through reaching out to her Hopi people and the Native Americans. She and her husband, Craig, host a weekly Bible study in their home for Natives in the Phoenix area, and it has been growing rapidly. Gerri has a gift of teaching.

All four of these people have wonderful testimonies. The Lord has also provided a mighty prayer intercessor, Betty Galusha, from Santa Barbara. She is an elder at our home church, and she really felt that the Lord was sending her to go with us that she may pray for the team. We are so grateful to our Lord for this.

The Initiations of the kids in the kivas

The Bean Dances, which recur yearly, will be happening in Hotevilla and Shongopavi this weekend. A male, dressed in white as a female kachina, will sing a lovely song before the dawn for the bean sprouts. There will be kids initiated in the kivas, and the children will come up out of the kiva after being whipped by a kachina at the end of the few days. Once again, I hear that some of my Sunday School children will be getting initiated in the kivas.

A Simple joy of being together

I am always in awe of the beauty of the Lord every day. And I thank our Lord that He is such a magnificent God that He has given us such a great privilege not just to be blessed in our lives, but TO BE A BLESSING to others and to the nations!

I have found this past year that almost all my works do not please God as much as when I am home to cook regular dinners for our children, and my husband, and to simply care more for my family. We have found a simple joy of sitting and eating and fellowshipping much more, together as a family around the table. We are so blessed to have such wonderful kids! Naphtali and John had thirteen others join them for a weekly "Kids for Christ" Bible study at Hopi High this week; this is truly a miracle in Hopiland for every week the kids continue to come.

We have been here over four years now. All who were in Hopiland when we first arrived have left the reservation. In fact during that time we have seen over thirty Christian workers come and go from this tiny reservation.

We were on the White Mountain Apache Reservation a couple weeks ago. We were blessed to go and pray with some of the pastors and the Chairman and the Vice-Chairman of that tribe. The Lord is bringing together His people to pray in unity. We just came back from YWAM "Harp & Bowl" Worship Conference in Prescott. We thank John & Kathleen Cooke who hosted the conference, and Bob Fitts who sang so beautifully. But we thank the Lord mostly for the prayers which were fervently sent up for the Hopi and Native American nations during this conference.

The Ainus of Japan

We are seeking the Lord about going to visit the Ainu people in Japan when we are in Korea. The Ainu were the last people group that the Lord showed us in Will's series of dreams. The dream was about a man wanting to adopt a child of a woman standing before him. In the end, he raised his hands to the heavens and cried out "Ishi!" Ishi in Japanese means "a stone or a pebble, will or volition, or a heart's desire." It is the name for "man" amongst the Yahi Indians of Northern California (see the book, Ishi) and it means man or husband in Hebrew (see Hosea 2:16). We think it may refer to God's spirit of adoption somehow touching the lives of these people in Japan.

We did not know at that time that there were any indigenous peoples in Japan other than the Japanese themselves. But afterward we discovered that there are the original people called the Ainus, and that they had been pushed up to the north of Hokaido. This is really just like the Natives around the world who have been pushed out of their homelands to some of the hardest regions. We don't even know whether we can get in to see them. We are in touch with

129

a friend in Montana who has worked closely with the Blackfoot tribe, and had heard that the Bear Clan from the Ainu nation was coming to meet with the Bear Clan in the Blackfoot tribe. The Hopis also have a Bear Clan which is the "priesthood" clan here in Hopiland. We would like to know whether the Lord is saying this is the time for any connections. I have not been in Korea for over 35 years, and I need to spend time with some of my long neglected family there also.

Being Blamed for New Christian Expressions

At the end of our YWAM Native Ministries Conference in January, our good Hopi Christian friend played a Hopi rattle at a church in Hopiland. The rattle had been made by a young Hopi

At the Gathering of the Nations in New Mexico

Christian man from one of the villages. A Native American hand drum had been introduced also as an instrument that could give worship to God. Now we understand that some other Christian leaders desire to get together in Winslow to have a meeting to blame us, saying that we have brought these new expressions.

Uberta, the widow of Pastor Daniel Quimayousi told us of this meeting. She also said that she had a dream where she was trying to work with a small ineffective little hand saw. Daniel, her deceased husband showed up in her dream, replacing the small saw in her hand with a huge sword, saying to her that she now needed the sword to fight. While we were driving to Flagstaff together, she told me that she thinks she knows why she had that dream. She said that she will go to go to the meeting to speak up and fight for us. She said, "I know your heart."

It is the belief that all native drums are demonic because some in the past were used to call up spirits. I could hardly blame them as it seems that this is all they knew as they have been taught long ago by the white missionaries. In Hopiland, it seems that if the Christians go against this belief that it would be betraying not just those faithful missionaries who brought Christ to them, but also their parents and grandparents who paid such a high price to leave all their native ways to follow Christ. And I could understand now also, how difficult it is that someone is saying that they could now choose for themselves. One elder sighed and said, "Before, they told us that we cannot speak our language nor do anything Hopi, and now they are telling us that we can."

Yes, it is confusing sometimes, but as the babies are born and grow, there are bound to be some messes to clean up. As these new believers are born and growing, we must not say that they should not have any messy diapers, for the church at large is not perfect either. One native friend said, "Why doesn't the church clean up what is bad within their white culture before they tell us to clean up ours?"

131

We have not brought the drums; the drums for all native people have been around as long as the natives and the animals have co-existed together on this earth. And the men had the ability to make the drums as long as they had deer, buffalos and seals. We were all meant to praise our God with our instruments as Psalms told us to do. We have an innate desire in all of us to worship. There must have been some good Native Americans who sang songs to our God on their drums even though they may not have known the name Jesus. How sad I am that this one matter would bring so much hurt and division amongst us as believers.

Oh sing to the LORD a new song!
For He has done marvelous things;
His right hand and holy arm have gained Him the victory.
The LORD has made known His salvation;
His righteousness He has revealed in the sight of the nations....
All the ends of the earth have seen the salvation of our God.
Shout joyfully to the LORD, all the earth;
Break forth in song, rejoice, and sing praises. - Psalm 98

How sad it is that the same religious spirits which brought so much "law" during Jesus' days on earth are still so active. The Law only seems to bring condemnation and division. It was the Pharisees who were so concerned with the law that they rebuked Jesus for healing the blind and the sick, and another time, plucking the wheat grain to eat on Sabbath.

They were so concerned with the law that they would have been against Jesus for going through Samaria and speaking to the woman at the well. They were angry that Jesus spoke, first of all, to Samaritans, for Jews did not associate with them as the Samaritans were considered to be like dogs to the Jews, and yet Jesus did. Secondly, the Pharisees would have been upset that Jesus spoke to women for Jewish men did not speak to women in public, but Jesus did. Thirdly, they would have said that it was absolutely preposterous that Jesus talked to this woman who had five husbands, but Jesus did anyways. It seems that Jesus was more concerned about the heart condition of this one Samaritan woman than all the laws which would have prohibited Him from doing what He did. Jesus did not consider his own reputation.

We cannot be less than who we are in Christ. For us to say that a Native American believer must play only a guitar or a Yamaha drum and sing only out of the old white hymnals, would be very offensive to our God. If we want to consider our reputation, it would solve many of our problems by switching over to telling the new believers in Hopi to cut everything of their culture.

This matter reminds me much of Paul's struggle with the Judaizers who wanted the new Gentile believers to practice Mosaic Law. These Judaizers followed Paul everywhere telling the converts that they must now all be like the Jews. They insisted that every male be circumcised. But, the Word of God makes it very clear that it is not about circumcision. In this case, we need to look at circumcision as what the white church is trying to insist saying that the new converts amongst the Native Americans now have to circumcise all of their culture, lock, stock and barrel. No culture is perfectly pure; therefore, it is not to say that one is not to cut off something of their culture, but not indiscriminately, all.

No outsider can possibly know everything about someone else's culture. There are over five hundred nations, recognized and unrecognized, within our nation. One tribe does not know what goes on in another tribe. And yet, the white denominational churches are still coming into the reservations, telling them to circumcise everything, including what may be honoring to God within their culture.

For in Christ Jesus, neither circumcision nor uncircumcision avails
anything, but faith working through love (Galatians 5:6)

...circumcision is that of the heart, in the Spirit, not in the letter...
(Romans 2:29)

Since there is one God who will justify the circumcised by faith and
the uncircumcised through faith, do we then make void the law
through faith? Certainly not! On the contrary, we establish the law.
(Acts 3: 30, 31)

Circumcision is nothing and uncircumcision is nothing, but keeping
the commandments of God is what matters. (I Corinthians 7:19)

Jesus said, "You shall love the Lord our God with all your heart,
with all your soul, and with all your mind. This is the first and great
commandment. And the second is like it. You shall love your
neighbor as yourself. On these two commandments hang all the Law
and the prophets." (Matthew 22: 37-40)

I do understand that it is not the arguments of the theologians that
solve the problems of a questioning heart.

The Sundays are the hardest

There was a Ladies Society Dance in the village of Hotevilla
on this Sunday. Not one Sunday School child came from Hotevilla,
only two from Kykotsmovi. There were so many cars in the village
because of the Dance that one could not drive to pick up the ladies
in the church.

Sundays can be very hard and discouraging. Between
picking up all the children in the villages, leading worship, Sunday
School, and then, once again, picking up the children for the Video
Night and snack shop and take them home, it takes more than 8
hours. I only have one friend my age that comes to church on

Sunday mornings. Sharon had received the Lord with us while she was at the Hopi Jail facility, and now brings her two girls from Kykotsmovi to church; she has been, for almost a year, a joy and encouragement to me.

I believe Sundays are the hardest for me and many other missionaries. In fact, a few of the other missionaries leave the reservation to attend a church in Flagstaff 100 miles away.

Mesa Verde
There are two kivas (see the ladders) that are actively used by pueblo peoples

Chapter 12

The Butterfly Dance

The Butterfly Dance will be held at the village of Old Oraibi, which is right above our home village of Kykotsmovi at Third Mesa, this coming weekend. Old Oraibi is generally known as THE oldest continually dwelt-in settlement in all of North America. We are invited to these dances but, at this point, we do not feel the freedom to attend yet.

"White man's religion" not wanted

Hopi Jail ministry continues to go well. We know that some Hopi men and women have decided that they do not want to be any part of what they believe is "white man's religion". Many, however, continue to come, both men and women for they have found a true and meaningful connection with the Creator's Son.

This week, one young man told us that he has been reading the "Daily Bread" out loud to the other inmates. He said some don't like it but then he reads it to them anyway. This was after he had received the prayer of deliverance after coming to us in jail because of the strong demonic presence that he felt was tormenting him. This morning, our Christian brother who got out from the Hopi Jail, called our home, desiring to do his community service hours with us at YWAM.

Replacing a 100 year old church building

The last patriarch at Kykotsmovi Church has just passed away this morning. Lorenzo Yoyokie was in his 90's. And now there is only his son and several ladies who will sustain that church since Pastor Karl Nasawytewa also passed away last year. However, the Lord is up to something because last year they have started construction of a new church building that can possibly fit a few hundred people along with a brand new kitchen and Sunday School rooms. The church will be ready and there will be a dedication service on April 1. Why is the Lord, at this time, building this huge church (by the Hopi standard) to replace a small century old building that was ready to collapse? People are asking, "Who will come and fill this church building?" It is our prayer that the Lord is getting ready for a new harvest!

KUYI Hopi Radio station and the Gospel Hour

Now, for the first time, Hopi radio station called KUYI (means "water") has gotten off the ground. The ladies from Hotevilla and I were invited to come and sing on their first "opening" day. So here we went with my guitar and singing about Jesus in Hopi. God has been so good to give us so many opportunities to honor Him over and over again. Now, in spite of the hatred towards the "white man's Gospel," they are airing Hopi Gospel Hour music on Sunday mornings between 7:00-8:00 a.m.

Going back to Mozart and Chopin

I get in a rut some days out here in Hopiland. The other day, the Lord spoke quietly in my heart and said, "Go back to the things you love to do." So, I sat and listened to some operas and Mozart and Chopin's piano music to feed my soul. Yes, we need food for our soul and spirit, as well as for our body. I felt that I was sometimes holding my breath as I listened to Cecilia Bartoli singing those incredibly high and beautiful notes that almost seem to open Heaven's gates. I realized once again that we need to tend the gardens that God has given us. This means the garden of our heart and mind also. It is too cold to tend the flower garden out here in mid-winter, but we can tend other gardens of passion in our lives. I believe the Lord desires that for us.

No Sunday Church

No Sunday church service this morning up at Hotevilla. Uberta called and said that the roads are so bad that we can't drive to pick up anyone. It is true, after an overnight trip to Flagstaff with the Sunday School children, that our church van was swerving all over the muddy roads in Hotevilla as I was taking the children home; it is a wonder that we did not get stuck yesterday.

The Traditionalist and the Progressives

There is a prophesy in Hotevilla that if they give in to the white men's ways that the world will come to an end so there are no paved roads, no running water, and no electricity (but solar power is allowed). Some, however, are for these modern ways which brings much division amongst the "traditionalists" and the "progressives." All of the Hopi desert land is covered in snow this morning and it is predicted to snow all the way to midnight tonight.

Pastor Jo & Lily Curley

We have asked a Navajo pastor, Joe Curley, to go to Australia with us. He is in his 70's and has fought both in World War II and in the Korean War, and he walks with a limp from an injury which he suffered in Korea. We had fallen in love with this sweet old pastor and his wife, Lily, when they started attending our weekly prayer meeting for the missionaries at our home. As a little boy, Joe was adopted by a Hopi family and was raised up at Old Oraibi. We can see the Mennonite Church that was burnt down twice by lightning in Old Oraibi from our house. After the lightning destroyed the church the second time, it was not re-built.

Pastor Joe received Christ after ridiculing his wife for going to church every Sunday with their little children. One day to his surprise, after throwing the Bible across the room as Lily was running out the door to go to church, he found that he was hardly able to breathe. He said he was barely able to drive himself to the church and almost crawled up to the pulpit and begged to be saved, and there he received Jesus as his Lord and Savior.

Joe and Lily have been pastoring a church in "Teesto" in Navajo land, about a half hour from Hopiland, for many years. He wants to be able to go with us before he gets too much older, and wishes that his wife could go along also. (But we have not raised enough funds for this and it is such a short time before we leave that this would take a miracle!) They have adopted Will and me and call us their "son and daughter." They have been such faithful servants out in the middle of this desert land for so many years. Joe has what is called "no record birth certificate," and it looks like we can get an "emergency passport."

Chapter 13

All is Well, the Battle has Already Been Won

The ladies in our team will wear their "mantas" (traditional Hopi dress) when we go to Australia. A manta is a black dress with red and green ribbons or yarn sewn across the chest and below the knee area. The manta is worn when the girls get initiated into Hopi ways in the kivas, and in other ceremonies, but it was also worn long ago to do regular chores around the house. The ladies going on this team felt that the dress also had a redemptive story to tell. The black meaning that we are in sin, but the red ribbon would represent the blood of Jesus who cleansed us and the green representing our growth in Him.

Also on our tambourines, each of the ladies have painted drawings of Hopi symbols, which would represent the redemptive stories of God: Hopi rain cloud, Hopi rainbow, with raindrops between every row of colors, a butterfly, and an eagle will be on our tambourines when we play them to contemporary Native American worship songs. Gerri and I will also wear a "Butterfly headdress" which is a brightly colored painted piece. We want to show the Aborigines some of the beautiful culture of the Hopi ways. And we will tell them that we have been "Born again." May they see that following Jesus is not only a "white man's religion."

The ladies have spoken in three Hopi churches on recent Sundays, and there is a new excitement amongst the people here that now it is no longer enough for the missionaries to come to this land, but that now they are sending their own missionaries out to the nations. Yes, it is indeed a history-making time! And Jesus says, "All is well."

"All is well." This is what the Lord said to me as I was driving around to find Loretta in Flagstaff to bring her back to Hopiland for our Australia training. I knew there was a battle going on in the Heavenlies and that many were praying. I even went to Loretta's 16-year old son's high school, but Albert was absent that day. And yet, the Lord kept saying to me, "All is well." I am in control. The battle has already been won!"

Taking the support letter to the police & the bank

Pastor Curley and Lily have not come to the training. They are not going to Australia, but Loretta called at 5:00 AM saying, "I am still coming." She shared how discouraging her support raising experience had been. She said she even took her support letter to the police station in Flagstaff and that the police were trying to ignore her, and how she made them listen. She was in there so many times before she came to the Lord, that she felt they should know what God is doing in her life now. She told us of how she got laughed at by a bank teller when she showed the support letter; she said she had to repent for slamming her fist on the counter because the teller had laughed at her letter. When Loretta had called and asked the teller for forgiveness, the teller told Loretta that "No one had ever asked for forgiveness, and that she should not have laughed at such sincere effort."

In sharing her testimony further during our training session with our team, Loretta was sharing how it used to take more than one policeman to take her into the Hopi Jail when she was drunk. All the other female inmates feared her because she used to make such a loud racket when she was taken in. She said that she did not hesitate to take away anything from any other inmates such as pencils or shampoo, and they all used to hide things when Loretta would come into the jail.

I remember when I first saw Loretta coming into our Monday night church service at the Hopi Jail. There was something very beautiful about Loretta even though I would not have wanted to meet her in some dark alley. And the Lord told me in my heart to tell her that she would be a teacher some day and would tell many women about His love. Loretta could not believe those words. But already, she has done that in "Hope Cottage" Women's Shelter, and in other places.

We believe the Lord is having us take Loretta's son Albert with us on this Australia mission trip to the Aborigines. He had been left behind many times in his life, including being in five separate foster homes because of Loretta's mistakes in her life. This was before she knew Christ. I could see the anguish in Loretta and the intense battle not to give up her only son, not trusting anyone to take care of Albert, even for these few weeks. And yet finally, she, like Abraham, was willing to put her son down at the altar. Someone had asked whether we had considered Albert. No, we had not. He is the least of the clan. We were only interested in mature older pastors and men for our team. And yet, we sense that the Lord is up to something new. God seems not to be interested in the appearance of men but to choose the youngest of all the brothers, like little David, to kill the giant.

Albert is probably the only Hopi teenager who got baptized in the past 30 years or more in Hopiland. He was baptized with his mother last year. After all that he has gone through in his life, he has no anger or bitterness in him. He is this huge young man with every cell in his body filled with God's special grace. He has five Native blood lines running through him, including Hopi, Tewa, Laguna and Acoma. He would be representing these nations in Australia. Yes, it is time for Gen-X to come up; they will be the next generation to hold up the banners.

The "Block"

We have had such a great time with our new family in Red Fern and the area called the "Block", near Sydney. Our schedule was so full with hardly any time to rest. What was so obvious to us was that the Aborigines were not interested in hearing us, an Asian nor the whites, but they were all ears when our Hopi friends would share anything. There was a common bonding that took place between our Native American and Aboriginal friends as though they were long lost families and they were able to trust one another and hear one another's stories at another level.

That wasn't the end of His works in the Block. We had an amazing time of fellowship with pastors Billy and Kalene Simon, over dinner at their home. And Friday morning, we did an open-air service in the midst of Satan's seemingly ruined lives, again in the Block. The Lord showed up as the ladies danced, worshipped and spoke of His reconciliation and healing.

Nambucca Heads

We then proceeded up the coast further to our aboriginal friend Michael in Nambucca Heads. On the way, we stopped at a Koala breeding center. Loretta was in second heaven fulfilling dreams of a lifetime to be in Australia and to hold a kangaroo. The Lord is doing deep healing in her life.

The following was written by Will upon leaving: *Last Wednesday, we drove out of Nambucca Heads in the rain. We had*

143

prayed for sunshine and got three days worth. That morning we said goodbye to our hosts at the Murrbay Aboriginal Language Center where we had been staying.

A painting of the boomerangs by our Aboriginal friend in Nambucca Heads

It took a couple hours to break away. The people were overwhelmingly good to us. There was a very mixed group of local Aborigines, called Kooris. There were probably four or five elders, including Barry, the director, and Kenny, who had originally given us permission to stay here. They first presented us their language book with color pictures of their dream time heroes. And we responded by giving them a painting of a Hopi butterfly done by our Christian friend, Myron Beeson. Next they sang us a couple of songs and we responded in turn.

We first sang in Hopi and then in English, "Sing Hallelujah to the Lord," which speaks of Jesus being raised from the dead and coming back again. Millie had started that song. Initially, I was thinking that this was inappropriate, too in your face for people who don't necessarily have much good to say about their history with the church. But then I knew it was right, and sang wholeheartedly. Next I (Will) felt the Spirit guiding me to share my testimony.

We next drove up the street to Michael's home where we prayed with him and his wife Jennie. Millie prayed with her again to clarify her born again status with Jesus, after the previous night's prayer with her whole family. In the midst of that prayer a whole chorus of Kookaburra birds rang out with heavenly joy and laughter. Needless to say, we drove home praising and exalting God for all that He had done in Nambucca Heads!

A mural of an Aboriginal man right across from the railroad station in the "Block" near Sydney, Australia

Chapter 14

Songs for the Heart and Renewed Hope
(An excerpt from Will)

I've been back in Hopiland three days now, suffering from major jetlag. Initially, I struggled with the transition of being back, but yesterday morning, while driving the Mission School bus, the Lord gave me songs for my heart and a renewed love for this land and its people. He's doing wonderful things, though the challenges are many right now.

Pray please for people coming into the Rez this weekend to speak against native forms of worship. We have first-hand proof that God wants to bless indigenous worship. We have seen lives blessed and God glorified. Our hope is that these people, not so different from Paul's Judaizers (Act 15), will be won over by love and respect. They don't have to join us in indigenous worship, but they can choose not to fight us – and perhaps even bless us. We desire to bless them in doing all that glorifies Jesus.

A Litmus Test for Orthodoxy (from Will)

Last night, we had the beginning of a two-day workshop conducted by a native Christian organization based here in Arizona. I came in with a very open mind to hear their concerns about the place of Native culture within Christianity. By the end of this first meeting, I could see that it was the old religious spirits again pointing fingers at those who think differently from them, and demanding uniformity of belief by everyone else. They have taken a peripheral concern about how natives conduct worship and made it their litmus test for orthodoxy. And unfortunately, many of the older Christians here are not well grounded in their faith so these things just serve to confuse them and polarize the Hopi church at large.

Please pray with us! Pray that truth will prevail and that our freedom in Christ will not be stolen by legalistic demagoguery. Pray that these religious spirits would be bound, and that Hopi believers would stand for the grace they share in Jesus through faith.

Millie called me from Korea a couple days ago. She is doing well and will return on April 30. It makes this land a good bit drier without her here. Our kids are doing well also. We had a new YWAMer, Virginia Humphreys, doing her two-month DTS outreach, from YWAM Perth, here with us. She has been a real blessing.

Mother's Day Luncheon

Lavender and sky blue table cloths, pink and white balloons, hot pink napkins, oriental fans and red Carnations awaited our Hotevilla ladies for the Mother's Day luncheon on Sunday. We had a lovely time. It was VERY GOOD to be back home!

147

Korea: I could not handle another bowl of rice

Going to Korea was a wonderful treat, but I have no attachments there. My home is in Arizona. Our extended family there was so loving and gracious in treating us like royalty. It was very good to see some of the ancient palaces. My family hosted us with banquets in their homes and at restaurants, but I didn't know how Americanized I was until I could no longer handle seeing another bowl of rice with spicy Korean dishes for breakfast, lunch, and dinner. How I longed for pizza, hamburgers, tacos, and Italian food!

I had thought Korea was such a great Christian nation, but I was surprised and grieved to see so many Buddhist temples and those who were still bowing down to these statues. I desperately wanted to stop the people who were bowing over and over again before these Buddha figures in different squares. Oh, how very sad this was that they do not know intimacy with the living God.

I remember when I was taken to the Buddhist temples by my maternal grandmother when I was little. She was really my great-aunt. My mom's parents got stuck in the North during the Korean War. My mother was told by her parents that she should flee with her older brother to South Korea first, and that they would pack some more of their possessions and come down later. However, the border was closed soon after my mom and uncle had crossed into South Korea, and my mother never heard from them again. We do not know whether they are alive or dead or starving as North Korea is the darkest communist nation in the world. So, her aunt became my grandmother, and as I was the first grandchild, I became her favorite.

My grandmother would make me stand in the back of the temple and watch her bow and bow until she would finally murmur, "Oh, I cannot bow anymore," as she would reach over with her hand to her aching back. To this day, I have a hard time with the pungent

148

smell of incense as it reminds me of how I felt so empty in that temple, in my heart.

*It was always my dream to have a place
right by a stream or a creek.
The Lord took me out to the high desert instead.
I found a beautiful life amongst very wonderful people.*

My grandmother finally came to know Jesus in her life in her seventies. I had written to her, while in college, saying that Buddha was a good teacher but never claimed to be God and that if he was so wise, I wondered whether Buddha would have also worshipped Jesus if they had met on earth. I asked her to receive Jesus into her heart. She had been in Buddhism all her life since she was born, and also her parents. My grandmother was so angry with me that she cut me off. This hurt me greatly as she always sent letters to me. Even when she got too old to write, she recited her letters to her maid who wrote them down and sent them to me.

Then, finally, I received a letter from Korea, after almost fours years of not hearing from her. I was trembling as I went into my room to open it. She said she knows Jesus now and goes to Church all the time and that she has joy that she had never known before. I loved her so much that I felt Heaven would not be heaven for me without her. I had begged the Lord to reach her so many times! I fell on my knees weeping and thanked Him with all my heart.

200 Deep purple Irises in my Garden

I realized my home is where God has me, and that God had brought us to Hopiland. I was greeted by almost 200 deep purple flowering Irises inside my fenced-in garden in front of our home, with a painted gate that says, "God bless all those who enter here." The Irises had bloomed while I was not looking, and my only apple tree which I planted is so much taller now. Soon, I will be able to sit under it to be able to read my Bible.

Hopi girls' Softball team sang, "Light the Fire"

While going down to Phoenix on the Hopi High School bus, one girl asked Naphtali whether she could teach her the song which she had heard somewhere, called "Light the Fire." This girl, then, asked the other girls on the bus to learn this song as well. The song talks of how their spirit is hungry but that their flesh is weak. It says that the Lord knows where they have been and cries out to God to light the fire and to fan the flame in their hearts and to make them whole.

Later in the year, we had Mr. Wirth, the Hopi High girl's softball coach and his wife over for dinner in our home. He said he simply could not believe that he was hearing a bus full of Hopi girls singing all these Christian songs for so many hours. Later, when some of these girls ran into Naphtali at the High school, they would sometimes sing it out loud in the hallways.

While Naphtali was sitting outside of her room at the Hotel, reading her Bible, her coach asked Naphtali to come into her room to tell her about what she was reading. Soon, some other girls knocked and came in and said, "We want to hear too." When Naphtali went back to her room, the girls asked why she was gone so long. Naphtali told them that they were talking about God. The girls said, "Why don't you tell us? We want to hear!" On their way back home, Naphtali said she could not believe how many hours this softball team sang on the bus, songs like, "Lord I lift Your name on high," and "Humble thyself in the sight of the Lord."

To be a Speaker at the Graduations

Naphtali will be giving a speech at Hopi High graduation ceremony in front of a few thousand people. She has also been asked to be the honored speaker at the 6th grade graduation commencement at Hopi Mission School. May our Lord Jesus be glorified all the way on both of these days in Hopiland. She has, like her sister, received a four-year full scholarship to Northern Arizona University, but hopes to go to YWAM Discipleship Training School in Australia first.

"The love of my life"

"I would also like to acknowledge the love of my life – Jesus Christ. I love Him more than anything in the world. He has given so much to me and He has always been good! The peace that He gives when you're feeling scared, depressed, or happy is indescribable, or as the Bible says, "He gives peace which the world cannot give or even understand."

These words of Naphtali, our daughter, rang out through the loud speakers at the 2001 Hopi High School graduation, and the Lord was glorified. Naphtali gave two separate speeches that day as

Naphtali on the 1ˢᵗ page of Hopi Tutuveni (which means "paper" in Hopi) Newspaper

152

the Student Body President and as the Salutatorian, and received three separate awards. I heard a lady who was sitting behind me on the bleachers say, "Gee, that girl is getting all the awards."

The Hopi Tribe presented her with a laptop computer at this graduation. I was always amazed at the generosity of this Tribe who treated our kids with such kindness even though they were not Hopi. No one could deny that Naphtali had a mighty God. I believe the Lord made her a star that day because she dared to give Him the highest honor, as the love of her life.

Children's ministry workers' workshop

Before leaving us, Virginia, conducted a Children's Ministry Workers class at our YWAM facility. How we need to reach the children regularly in this land. There are no Sunday Schools in any of the villages other than in Hotevilla and at the Polacca Assembly.

We were invited to an Alaskan Native Christian gathering by Lynda Prince, who is so important in the Native Christian movement in the present days. Even though we had just come back from international travel and my head spun at the thought of leaving again, we sensed such an excitement in our hearts that we believed we were supposed to go. I believe God is moving at a rapid pace!

Our children are all out of the house

As far as leaving our children, both Clover and Naphtali are out of the house, and our 16-year old son, John, will be at Harvard University with the Hopi High School Science and Medical Program for three weeks later this summer.

John is gone now to do a YWAM Niko Wilderness Program in Salem, Oregon. After being on a White Water River rafting trip with the Korean youth, he felt convicted by the Lord that he is to carry on the mantle of continuing the "KFC" (Kids for Christ) group at Hopi High School this coming school year. But he felt he needed to be trained more and get stronger in the Lord so he decided to follow these Korean youth who were going to the Niko Wilderness School. So now Will and I have an empty nest. How strange! It seems they were all just babies the other day.

Even the rocks will smile if we don't!

Chapter 15

An Invitation to Alaska's Gathering of the Eagles

We have received a personal letter of invitation from Lynda Prince, a Native from Canada and the Grand Chief of her tribe. She said that she would like to invite us to The Gathering of the Eagles in Minto, Alaska. It will be a history in the making type of gathering as we merge first nations and Israel together in Turtle Island. She said in her letter that Minto was chosen to host this historic event as it has had a prophetic destiny. When the gospel first came to the village of Minto, its shamans all renounced witchcraft, burned their fetishes and converted to Christ. Its people have had visions and divine visitations for years, and she believes that some of their visions will come to pass at this gathering!

Also significant is that the eldest traditional chief of the Athabascans, who is over 100 years old still lives here. Lynda reported in this letter that he had recently died, and came back to life for the Lord said that he could not come home yet as Israel was coming and they had to be received! Wow!

Lynda urged us to come if we could take the time out of our schedule. She said that the Minto community will feed traditional food to their guests for the entire four days. She asked us to pray, as we labor to do things YAH's way and bring the glory back to Turtle island!

120 Native American Drums

In 1998, Lynda Prince had a vision from the Lord to have 120 drums made and dedicated to Jesus. When these hand drums were taken to Israel, the Native Christian drummers were not only welcomed by the Israeli people, but they were even invited to the Israeli

A Native American hand drum

Parliament! This was during the time when missionaries in Israel were being asked to leave. These same 120 drums will be in Minto, Alaska. I believe that the Native American Christians will be one of the people groups that will bring a revival to the Israeli nation!

There were three separate Kachina dances in Hopiland on different mesas this weekend. In Kykotsmovi, from my home, I could hear the drums beat from very early morning to late into the night from the plaza. The drumbeats are very important to the Hopi nation. Oh how we need the drums that would beat for our Lord Jesus Christ! Perhaps, some day, the 120 drums will come here.

It was truly exciting to be in Minto, Alaska! How wonderful our God is! He gave us a glimpse of heaven. To me, to hear these drums, dedicated to Jesus, being played all at once was like hearing the heart of Jesus Himself. And it was as though every beat was breaking the bondages and chains in the heavenly realm, calling the

First Nations' people to come to Him, to be children of God and to know the marvelous inheritance in Him.

I was so impressed with the love of God from all of the three Grand Chiefs, Will Mayo, Lynda Prince, and Kenny Blacksmith, who were there. There was so much dignity and honor and yet humility. I saw what our mighty Lord can do with the First Nations' people. He means to fulfill the word, "The first shall be last, and the last shall be first." Yes, He is saying the native people around the world had been oppressed and pushed down, but that now He is raising them up in dignity and power to be honored and welcomed by many other nations to bring the Good News of our Lord Jesus Christ.

It was also exciting to me to find out after talking to Will Mayo (the Grand Chief of all the Athabascan nations) that he had gone to speak to the Ainu people in Japan. It is just one more link God was confirming to me that He has a plan to reach the native people around the world as He had shown us in the dreams.

We have found out that these Native Christians are going all over the world to spread the Gospel. Lynda Prince was welcomed by the Queen of England, as well as the Parliament of Israel, twice with the 120 drums. Why is it that she is able to get an audience in places that most of us would never be invited to? It is because the people around the world are fascinated by the Native Americans. It does not seem to matter that the drums have Christian symbols and Bible scriptures on them. The whole world seems to want to hear and see the Native Americans with their incredible array of regalia, feathers and songs. These First Nations followers of Christ are being honored everywhere they go.

The only strange thing about being in Alaska was to come out of the meetings after midnight or at 2:30 AM and to find it still light and to see all the children playing on the playground. As I said, when the gospel first came to Minto, its shamans all renounced

157

witchcraft, burned their fetishes and converted to Christ. When Will Mayo first came to preach the Good News, kids 5 years to the oldest youth were having prayer meetings until six in the morning, prophesying and having visions. And now, the people of Minto are praying about the finances to go to Israel to bring the Good News of Jesus.

The people of Minto had been so wonderful to us. They fed us and made us feel welcomed in their beautiful lakeside land. It was fabulous to hear them singing and welcoming us in their own language, and to see the ladies getting up and dancing side to side in a rowing motion as they worshipped the Lord. This 'Hope" is what I sensed for the Hopi nation now. If God can do it there, God can do it here! I am so much in love with our everlasting Creator and the incorruptible seed of His Good News.

Sometimes I feel like my Apple tree

I know in my heart that I desperately want to seek God and be the kind of woman He wants me to be. Sometimes I wonder what we have accomplished.

There will always be someone against us when we follow Jesus, but I believe that even though we are going through persecutions that the Lord has given us favor through many Hopi families and friends. Otherwise, we would never have been able to get to acquire a large building on the major highway, which goes right through Hopiland. And the Hopi Tribe would not have brought the Island Breeze group themselves through us, and we would not be able to stay in our house in Kykotsmovi. Even so, I get so discouraged at times that I feel like my apple tree in my garden in this harsh desert land with the wind strong enough to be like sand paper abrading it, the locusts eating it, hot heat melting it, and thorny bushes growing around the roots taking the living water from it.

A resplendent tree glowing in the light, south of the Mogollon Rim.
It thrives in harsh winds and rocky soil.

I say, "What is the purpose of living for the Lord?" on one hand, and yet I know there is no other choice to make but to do the things God wants me to do while I live on this earth. I think if it was not for my garden, I may go mad out here sometimes. I sit and wait for the Lord's presence in my garden under my apple tree, planted three years ago. Now it has gotten tall enough to pass the roof of our house. And then, He comes and says, "Why are you so discouraged and downcast?" I do desire to serve the Lord with all my heart and all my might while I am still living, more than anything else.

A Ludicrous idea

I don't understand what the Lord meant when he said to me, "200 Koreans in Flagstaff," but only that we must seek to do our best to find out and to do as the Lord said. And I don't understand what the Lord meant when he said to Will, "Build a stable university." A YWAM University of the Nations? What a ludicrous idea this is if it was from our own heads! Who wants to do such a thing and would think of such a far-fetched idea? We did not know then that we would soon start doing Discipleship Training Schools and that the other schools will follow.

We felt it is wisdom to go slow, keeping a low profile. We did not feel the freedom to have a web page on YWAM Northern Arizona or Hopiland. But, even without it, we have had so many people who wrote and called saying that the Lord has given them a burden for the native people. Having three YWAM families here in Hopiland can be stretching the "law of invasion," but most of the Hopi people seem to feel that we are a benefit to their nation. We know from all that has been shown to us that we are to extend to Flagstaff one day.

The Grand Canyon, which is only two and a half hours from Flagstaff and Hopiland, is considered by many to be the most impressive natural wonder in the world. I believe that God will supply the staff and students as we move in His footsteps. I know for myself, I had come to Hopiland saying I could be here for the rest of my life, my ambition being that we would serve the Lord here. We had no big ambition for Flagstaff, but I believe this is the Lord's doing. We believe we ought to look for a YWAM property in Flagstaff country but still have a base here in Hopiland where we can minister and pray.

We have seen many, many miracles and we know God can provide what He desires for us. We have also seen the headache of having a facility, and renting as well. We would not choose to enlarge ourselves if we did not see it as a mandate from the Lord, for too many headaches and heartaches can come with properties.

Sea & Summit in Fort Defiance and in Hopi

Will and our kids, Clover and John, are out doing a Sea & Summit outing with 30-50 Navajo kids in Fort Defiance right now. Both the village of Mishongovi and the Hopi Youth Counseling program have signed up to do Sea & Summit trips this summer. Also, a Korean Youth group is coming out to join some of the Hopi youth to partner and go white water river rafting with our Sea & Summit program.

Yet another death

One of my Sunday School boy's mother was found dead in her room where she went to work at the Grand Canyon – yet another death out here. I cry for the loss of his mom, he had played Joseph in our Christmas play at the church.

It was very good to spend time with the boy who lost his mother. We read John 14 together about how Jesus went to prepare a place for us. I will lose him as he is going to New Mexico to live with his dad. I lose many children from Sunday School when there are dances or ceremonies at any of the villages around the calendar year, or if the parents move out of Hopiland to look for a job, or when they get initiated in the kiva, as almost all the children do. And yet, I am seeing that now more kids are coming back to church even when they have been initiated. God is good!

"He will not discourage," it says in Isaiah 41. Furthermore, He says, "A bruised reed He will not break, and a smoldering wick, He will not snuff out. I, the Lord, have called you in righteousness. I will take hold of your hand." I am standing firm in this message!

Run, Tribalwinds DTS, Run!
We are with the Hopis- the long distance runners.

In 2009, Hopi High Boys' track team got 1st place in the State Championship,
making it twenty (yes, twenty) straight years in a row!
The girls' team won 1st place in the state, three years straight.
It is amazing when a team wins the championship just once!

A flute player painting by Fred Kabotie at the
Watch tower at Grand Canyon

I am sure Jesus was weeping too

It was hard to sit and listen to little "Cassie", who attends the Sunday School, cry as she was finally able to open up how she misses her aunt who was recently found murdered at the Grand Canyon. She said she wished God had not taken her aunt to Himself and that her mom couldn't stop crying. All I could do was just hold her next to me and cry with this little seven year old. I am sure Jesus was weeping, too. The joy is that Cassie's mother, who never comes to Church, was one of those who came to the "Day of Prayer" this past week.

In the past, when a Hopi died, two of the male relatives would tie prayer feathers to the one who died and place the fetal positioned body in the cleft of a rock and cover it with sand and then with rocks. Only those two would know where the body was laid. However, this practice is no longer done as there are not enough cliff side openings left on these mesas.

These days the bodies may be buried in the ground, still in a fetal position, and sand piled on top in a mound shape and flagstones put on top of the mound. Another traditional way we have seen is to dig a hole and then dig a small cave like hole in the side of the main hole. The body is then placed within that cave as above and flagstones are placed to seal off the hole. Then the main hole is filled back in forming a mound which is covered again with flagstones.

The third way we are aware of is to bury the body in a casket, which may have a hole in the lid to let the spirit out, and then the main hole is covered as before. Someone said that the stones are put so that no wild animals would be able to dig in to the body. The Hopis believe that after four days, the soul would start its journey back to Grand Canyon, to the Hopi afterlife in the underworld. During these four days, people are not supposed to talk about the dead as this may hold them back from going to their final destination. Also, there is a fear that a bad spirit may attach itself to anyone who touches the dead body.

Much Happenings in our village

My neighbor across the street, Lucille Namoki, a potter, just called asking me to take her up to the ancient village of Old Oraibi, to take her pottery to be fired. I rarely get to enter the village of Old Oraibi so I am excited to go with her.

We are having a very busy month. The Somer Haven group was at Hotevilla for a week, and we have a white water river rafting expedition with Hopi and Korean youth, from the Light of Love Church soon. Valley Baptist Church from Michigan has come to do Kid's Club at YWAM. Hotevilla Church Sunday School is doing an outing to the Water World in Phoenix with Word of Grace Church. Global Mission Church is at our YWAM building to do `Kids Club in Hotevilla, youth work in Second Mesa, and a Barbecue for the communities.

We also had an Awards Banquet for the Mishongovi Youth trip at our YWAM facility for those Hopi teens who went on the River rafting trip with Will. It was so great to have so many parents, grandparents and friends who have come and saw the fun experiences these young people were able to share.

Our home was a flurry of activities as soon as we came back from our week of vacation with our three kids. Our friend and an old staff person, Todd, who had been living in Switzerland with his Swiss wife, came to visit us for a couple of days. Our neighbor boy across the street came to our home this morning to go to Hopi High with John. Jonathan Eckstrom, the Bible translator, after his wife passed away a couple years ago, is engaged to be married and he and Marcia, his fiancée, were both at our home for dinner. Our neighbor, Merwyn, in his twenties, was back at church and hanging around our home again. And this afternoon, I had Merwyn's cousin who went on our Sea & Summit Expedition a few years ago), drop in so that I can fill out a reference form for her.

Also, we have three Korean interns through IMI Korean ministry who are applying to be in Hopiland for two months with us. There is so much need in the area of workers for the children and youth for every church out here, but it is only our Heavenly Father who can direct all of us to do His will.

Our Awards Banquet and Barbeque with the Substance Abuse youth from the Hopi Guidance Center went very well. They were able to see the slides of the Hopi-Korean youth river rafting expedition, and hear the excitement of the kids who went. Sea & Summit t-shirts were awarded by us, and a certificate by the Hopi counselor who went on the trip. Will is invited to come and speak with the head of the Hopi Guidance Center this week for they want to do more trips through Sea & Summit.

We are not supposed to be able to rent in Hopiland

Please pray for us as we have received a copy of the letter from the Hopi Tribe which was sent out to our landlady of our YWAM building. Apparently, an individual cannot lease any building to a non-Indian business. We are a "non-profit" but they consider us still a business. Marvin Yoyokie said that he would represent us if necessary, if there is to be a Tribal Council hearing. This building we are leasing has been sitting idle and deteriorating for nearly twenty years. It is rather strange that this letter is sent after the building has been resurrected, with much help from so many of our friends and Churches, and not before. And yet, we are so confident that the Lord will work out all things for good.

God has blessed us in many ways. But we are also going through some real trying times. I was even thinking, on our family vacation, how it might be nice to have an eight to five job again because the stress of being in the ministry can be pretty wearing on one's soul. (I am certain that many eight to five jobs are also very stressful) But, we recognize that our battle is not against flesh and blood, but of principalities and powers. And, we know how we can win this battle one day at a time! I am tremendously comforted to know the end of this chapter of the story and that we are on the side of the King who wins!

Our ministry base in Santa Barbara to be sold

We as the board of directors are wondering what to do with the YWAM Santa Barbara base. We spent months in prayer and pondering before the Lord. The Lord had spoken to our hearts in each of the other members on our Board that the base (which used to be called "Winterhouse") is to be sold. We had waited for the Lord to raise someone to take over the ministry there in Santa Barbara, but this was not to be.

Our board President went out to contact other qualified YWAM leaders to take over the base, but all who he had approached prayed and said that they are not called to work in Santa Barbara. Can you imagine that, no one wanting to come to a place only a few blocks from the beach? A town which is so beautiful that it had its own Soap opera called, "Santa Barbara" in U.S. and also in Europe. Once the property is sold, the board needs to decide how the proceeds are to be distributed. May the Lord be glorified in all this!

The Koreans- a colorful display of God's wonders

I think these Korean youth are a colorful array of God's wonders, and a fragrant scent of worship to our Lord. We have a Korean church here from Hacienda Heights, California. They have been such an encouragement to us. Many children have come from Hotevilla to be with these youth as "kids" club is being held every day. They seem so alive and look so much like the Hopi youth themselves

Zion Canyoneering

Tonight they are sharing their Korean dances, testimonies, praise and worship songs with body motions and even very "Hot" hip-hop routines for the younger generation at Hopi High School auditorium, at the invitation of a board member. Something good is happening. There is a little taste of a harvest; some who never would enter a church building in the past 5 years, are coming into the church.

Two Indigenous men huffing and puffing

Paul Otoko and Brian Brightcloud decided that they would go for a hike up to Old Orabi with me. It was really quite a site to watch this Micronesian/ Polynesian and an Apache brother puffing and huffing. They had to stop many times along the dirt road to catch their breath. I was not quite in shape myself, but I felt like a mountain gazelle compared to my two brothers whom, I believe, may have had way too much Fry Bread recently. I know they were both really muscular and fit men once upon a time. (By the way, this is a Native American form of humor, to make fun of one's brother or sister when one is fond of them.)

Once, he used to beat up on missionaries

The first time Paul went to a kiva was when one Hopi man, "Al," showed up at our YWAM facility in Kykotsmovi just when Paul happened to be there. The man was angry and a bit intoxicated. He was telling Will that we had no business being in Hopiland. He said that the Hopis have their own way.

He also kept insisting that he wanted to meet with our staff ladies next door. Mixed in to the disjointed conversation he said that he wanted to take Will and Paul to the ceremony that night at Old Orabi. Will said, "Yes let's go" in order to get him out of our base.

So that night, they drove up to Old Orabi together. After being shown two kivas, when Al got to the third one around midnight, he invited Will and Paul to go down into the kiva with him. Will followed Al, who was mostly sobered up, down the ladder. Paul thought Al was going to come back up the ladder so he could also go down, but Al never came back up to get him.

Paul stood in that freezing weather, outside the kiva, for almost two hours without a coat in the dead of winter. He was almost frozen like a Popsicle when they finally came back down to our house. He said he could see the eyes of the men staring at him through their masks (which the Hopi men call their "friends") as these different sets of kachinas passed down the big wooden ladder into the kiva. Paul said as he looked down from the entrance way, from the top of the roof into the kiva, that all he could see of Will was Will's knees and his shoes below, with Al next to him. He said later that as long as he saw Will's feet moving or tapping that he knew Will was still alive. Paul said that he felt he was not to go down into the kiva, but to simply stay behind to pray for Will and the Hopi people. Paul has always been like that to support others rather than trying to stand out himself.

Once, Paul used to beat up on missionaries on his islands. Now all he wants to do is to bring the love of our God wherever he goes, through their Island songs, dances and hard work, with all the young men and ladies who Paul is discipling and teaching.

Chapter 16

Cultivating My Garden in This Ancient Land

Tonight, I sat and watched the Milky Way and all the other beautiful stars in my backyard. I believe I have come to love the high desert as much as one can. I have strived to work hard in order to make a small botanical garden. There are pathways formed with rocks and small stones found on our property and elsewhere in Hopiland, and the perennial and annual flowers planted among the natural desert plants, which flourish in this land. I have found that if I am regular at hoeing out the little green tumbleweed sucklings, while they are just sprouting on our pathways, that the garden can be easily maintained. I have learned many lessons as I have come to cultivate my garden at our Kykotsmovi home. One of those lessons was that, with much persistence and vision, one can have a marvelous creation even in the dry high desert land.

I have been so encouraged with the Puhu qatsi (Good life) ladies group. Last night, a lady, who had been a medicine woman, came for the first time and shared how the Lord had been nudging on her heart to come. She did not know that Debbie and I had been praying for her on our weekly early morning prayer walks. Also, the Lord has a strange way of answering prayers. I was quite perplexed about the fact that I had not been able to really reach my neighbors, after 5 years, and began lifting them up with Virginia Yoyokie, also on our prayer walks. Well, the Lord brought both the mother and the daughter to "church," at the Hopi Jail, so that they may hear the Word of the Lord. God does not always answer the way we think.

10K Tewanima Race

Will is running the 10k Tewanima Race up at Shungopavi on Second mesa. Louis Tewanima was a Hopi man who was a two time Olympian in the early 1900's. Running is an important part of Hopi culture and spiritual life. Unlike the Western church, Natives do not separate the spiritual out from the more common activities of life. Biblically everything should be done with an orientation toward Jesus, but our culture resists that. Native cultures are saturated with their spirituality. So when the various villages sponsor a foot race it is also a spiritual event. The participants are running their prayers, similar to dancing their prayers, during ceremonies. Will has remarked on how special it is to be thanked by various onlookers as he runs. This is a race that attracts people from around the state and even internationally sometimes.

This race route goes from the ball fields in the village, down the mesa cliff side, around the base of the mesa to the eastern most side, and then steeply back up the 500 plus foot cliff trail. I love to watch the runners coming up this switchback trail. All the Hopi families are gathered there cheering. Will says that in the midst of the pain, it is a wonderful sight to be coming up the steep trail to the encouraging cheers of so many people. It is such a spectacular view looking out onto the broad high desert floor, with First Mesa jutting up like a big ship at sea. Off to the right, one can see the Hopi buttes and the mysterious looking Navajo black volcanic plugs.

When you've done all you can, then, STAND!

The Lord said, "When you've done all you can, then to STAND." Through some real trials recently, I felt as if the enemy got me to a point where I utterly felt that I was not a good leader, and that I was, in fact, no leader at all. And that I should just give up and that it would make everything easier for everyone including myself if only I would quit. I am amazed at how communications amongst the Christians can get so fouled up. It is like a virus on the computer, which we recently got infected with, and also ended up sending to others. It is also like our friend who called their 11-digit long distance carrier number and found themselves being connected to 911. However, after having done all I can, and then simply "standing," I am sensing hope once again, as I have been able to befriend the desert land and I have my Garden, a gift from my Father.

There is no sunset as beautiful as the ones in Arizona

The Lord is listening to every earnest plea

This morning, Virginia Yoyokie and I climbed to the top of the village of Old Oraibi right above Kykotsmovi. We climbed down the other side of the cliff side praying over the village, asking the Lord to forgive the sins of any idol worship, and to open the hearts of the people in Hopiland to see Jesus Christ as the answer to all their need for forgiveness for their lives. Yesterday, the three Korean interns went, as we do every Friday morning at 5:30 AM to pray; this time to the site near Mishongvi and Shipalavi. We prayed asking the Lord to have new mercies shower down on the Hopi people there. We believe that our prayers are effective and that the Lord is listening to every earnest plea.

Hopi quilts

The New Life ladies are interested in forming "Quilts For The World" (a project started by Sheila Meadows) at our YWAM building. They would like the first quilt that every group of ladies makes (worth $100) to go to the general fund so that they can buy new machines and other needed materials, and then split the other future sales between the workers to help their families.

We have been praying for five years for some kind of "economic redemption" in Hopiland because whenever Jesus goes into any nation, He brings economic healing, as well as the spiritual, emotional, and social redemption through His Gospel. The last quilt that was made had an eagle in the middle, two green corn stalks, and a Hopi rain cloud, as well as two Hopi pots.

Already six Hopi quilts have been ordered by different friends. We are still sorting through some business issues with the village and the Hopi tribe to make sure that we are starting this out right because we want to make sure that the Lord will be glorified from start to finish. Whether getting a "small business license" and having this be totally independent, or to open a separate account and bring this under our YWAM non-profit status are some of the few questions we have not yet answered.

KFC and the Songs of the Hopi men

With the help of the Korean interns, John continues to make sandwiches for sixteen kids. Today, he will read the Scripture from the book of Samuel and talk to the kids about how God has chosen each one of those students to stand up for Christ like David in the Bible. How amazing it is that these Hopi youth are showing up! (nine young men, and two girls last week.)

What an amazing thing to hear the songs which some of the Hopi men in jail have written! They have already written ten songs in their own language. And they do the drum beat with their hands on the dining hall table. One song is about II Corinthians 5:17. "Therefore, if any man is in Christ, he is a new creature." The old things have passed away. Behold, new things have come! Tonight, Will is in there with two of our DTS students for the men's discipleship program, at which only twelve men are allowed to come, in order to keep the group more intimate.

God is faithful

While Will was near Bishop, the transmission on his '91 Trooper has gone out again after five years. This meant that we are going to put this cost on our Visa card and the thought of being in debt was not very good. I am encouraged to know that our God has been so faithful all these years, and we will be encouraged.

With a great team effort, New Life ladies' group was able to raise $400 for the $600 worth of prizes, which we purchased for the Fall Festival; The rest will be raised by selling hamburgers and hotdogs at the Festival.

What does decorating have to do with God?

I wonder what cleaning up and decorating has to do with God when there is a war going one? We have just put in insulation on the walls in Clover's old room so that John can move in there. And John's old room, with a makeshift divider, has been painted and decorated to extend from our living room so that we can easily get our wood and coal from the backyard, but mainly to entertain bigger groups of guests more easily.

I re-count the years that have gone by here in Hopiland. I noticed this Sunday at Hotevilla Gospel Church that I have begun to use my magnifying reading glasses in order to lead songs out of small-lettered Hopi hymnals. My hair is turning noticeably gray in some spots. "To color or not to color" is the question. Dynicea, a little six-year old girl in my Sunday School when we first came, will be turning twelve soon.

Monument Valley, Utah is one of our favorite places, as we go through this valley to the San Juan river.

176

We're alive and doing well!

Naphtali was out getting our cat and heard a rattle sound in the middle of the night near our home and our overnight guests also heard the same sound. It is very possible that someone was singing their song, but recently it sure felt like we have been under some attack. Someone threw an egg at my car after I had just taken all the Sunday school kids home. But whether these things were all spiritual or simply the natural occurrences of life, I believe our Lord Jesus has been FAITHFUL, and the people have seen it!! We are alive and doing well, and we see new people coming to learn of Jesus after the church in Hopiland has been dying for so many years.

We have also had much opposition from those who spread false rumors about us. We have been told that we have been kicked out of Hopiland because we brought in native-sounding worship to the church. The rumor was that we had done a "Butterfly Dance" in Australia on our outreach; we don't even know how.

The Fall and Winter activities

We praise the Lord for this second annual Fall Festival. Last year, approximately 100 people showed up at our YWAM facility. This year, we are expanding. Over 120 hamburgers and hotdog dinners were sold. And our quilt, the top portion which was done by the ladies in one day, sold over 80 raffle tickets. And a lady with a Hotevilla address won!

As soon as the Korean interns left, I took off with Will and the DTS team from YWAM Bishop to a wilderness area in Utah, near the Arizona border. I felt very much blessed to see the Northern Lights that evening as we sat around the fire. This is how I met Will while doing a wilderness program through Sea & Summit so long ago, and it was so good to be back again sleeping and being with young people who want so much to learn about all the wonderful inheritance God has for them. John Cooke taught for five days with them in the wilderness.

David Moko, a Maori, the Director of a YWAM indigenous base in New Zealand, has recently been here. He spoke at our facility on Thursday night to the Hopis. We had a good turn out. Ron & Roberta Archer from IRC (International Reconciliation Coalition), who work with John Dawson's ministry, also were here in Hopiland.

Thanksgiving break-in

Our house was broken into in Hopiland while we were gone to spend Thanksgiving with our family in California. It was a terrible feeling to walk into a house with the back window broken in and the curtains moving in the cold winter breeze and seeing broken pieces of glass all over the floor and on our furniture. My guitar which I use to lead worship on Sunday mornings, Thursday night ladies group, and jail ministry is gone. Our VCR along with John's new electric guitar with speakers, and even the guitar John had borrowed from his youth leader, are all gone also. The stereo system, which John won at Hopi High for being a good student, is gone, along with another CD player in our own room. It is funny, however, that the thieves left our junk T.V. sitting in the middle of the Living room after they took it out of our cabinet. When the thieves don't want your stuff, you know it is not worth much.

We are grateful that this does not seem to be a hate crime. They could have broken in and ruined many other items, such as our pictures and small antiques and other decorations, but they were in perfect order. However, this seems to happen to us about every year and a half. This time, I feel more sad and violated and wounded in my spirit. My heart feels rather cold, like the current temperature in Hopiland, with the melting snow on the ground.

Our house is pretty isolated and, if anyone is doing things at our back door area, no neighbor can see what goes on. And yet, we do not desire to bar up our windows and doors like a prison. The police have come out and took some fingerprints. The last time, along with many items, John's brand new Christmas gift, which some of the youth group had taken up a collection to buy, was taken. I feel angrier when our kids have suffered wrong.

However, we have been very much blessed; more blessed in every way than having suffered injustice. I did not go into the Hopi Jail ministry last night. The Lord, our God, is a good God and I desperately need His loving heart right now.

Our DTS (Discipleship Training School) at Grand Canyon

Chapter 17

A Rock Through Our Window at Our Home

Someone threw a rock through our window at 4:00 AM on Saturday. It is somewhat of a miracle that only one section of the glass on my small antique china cabinet was shattered, breaking only one saucer out of about forty tea cup sets I had. It seems rather amusing to me that God should care for these English tea cups that I have collected throughout the years and some that others had given to me. The rock was thrown so hard that it jammed the cabinet door, but how much worse it would have been if the rock was thrown into a bedroom and hurt our son John or Will. Our God is so good to protect us! We do need prayer for the culprit.

We have loved a young man like a son, but we had to call the police the last few times he had visited us. We have thought of the demon that comes back with seven other demons after seeing that his old house is swept clean.

However, just as the enemy is trying to bring seven other demons, there is a spiritual war going on in the heavenlies for God's beloved newborns in Hopiland. It is truly exciting to see some of our new Hopi brothers and sisters coming to the Lord and getting stronger in Him. Will is taking yet another young man to a Christian Drug Rehab Program in Phoenix next week, and another young man is waiting to enter the one in Bakersfield.

We are seeing that we are not going to win this battle out here alone. We need your prayers. I believe prayer is the only way some of them may remain sober and be protected from the enemy who wants desperately to pull them down.

Kicked out for refusing to cut his hair

Our Hopi friend whom Will drove out to California for a Christian Drug Rehab Program has been kicked out because he had refused to cut his hair. It saddened and angered me deeply for it seems this is exactly what the White Government and the Christian Church had done to the Native Americans at the boarding schools around 1860-1950. All the natives not only had to lose their own native language, dress, and culture, but had to cut their hair to look "white" and civilized Does cutting hair make one more of a Christian? Did we not learn this lesson a hundred years ago that we cannot do this again?

It is understandable that a program has to have some policies. And on one hand, I could understand that it is their program and much prayer and consideration may have gone into making these policies; it is certain that the policy makers thought these were beneficial for all concerned. And yet, this matter hits too close to the wounding of the Native Americans in our history. I can understand why our friend refused it and was kicked out. The counselor called us saying that our friend had left the program yesterday. And we are left not knowing whether we can continue sending any more of our new Hopi believers to this Christian program. Either they are very ignorant of our U.S. history, or they refuse to bend in this area. Is there any help for our newborn brothers and sisters from Hopiland with alcohol and or drug addiction? We are so concerned for our friend who is now out on the streets. He has not called us. Perhaps, he thinks that we may get mad at him for leaving that place. He does not have any money to get home and we could only now pray.

We have now learned weeks later that our friend who had been kicked out of a Christian drug rehab program had found his way over to his sister's home, four hours from where he was out on the street. We are glad he is safe. He says that he really enjoyed the Bible studies and other activities there and wants to enter another Christian program that would allow his long hair. Will and I have gone and talked with the Director of this same program, only in Phoenix this time. He understands the sensitive history of the Native Americans regarding the hair, but explained how they could not make exceptions for every nationality. We have talked about perhaps using much of their basic ideas, with a vision to create a program which may be more sensitive to the Native people group so that they would not fall by the wayside on smaller issues such as hair length. We want to bless this program and now recognize that we are all parts of the body of Christ, to serve differently.

From every Angle, the Enemy works

One of my most consistent Sunday School students told me this past Sunday that she will not be coming to church much longer. She said she was told by her grandmother that, if the Hopis went with the Christians, something bad will happen to her village. We need prayers to break these sorts of lies of Satan who continues to spread fear and false rumors amongst the people. We need prayer that the Holy Spirit will open the eyes of the Hopis to see that Satan is out to kill and destroy their people, but that only the love of Christ will bring them safety and deliverance.

It seems that Satan works from all angles, e.g., legalistic Christian philosophies to fear mongering ideas from Hopiland. Pray for God's move of the powerful anointing to help our new Hopi brothers and sisters and the Native people around the world to come to know and grow in Christ without so much hindrance.

One to one Counseling in Jail

As I am writing, Will is presently at Hopi Jail. He is counseling with a Hopi young man. It does not cease to amaze us how God is continuing to break through in Hopiland. Hopi Jail visiting hours are often only 5-10 minutes for the families, after waiting in the lobby for 2-3 hours twice a week. However, we have been given special permission to be able to sit with the inmates and counsel for one or two hours regularly. How amazing our Lord Jesus is to let the Hopi Tribe, who had been so resistant to Christ in the past, now open these doors so wide to us! Once, Will was confronted by a Detention Officer as to his qualification for doing counseling. I praise the Lord that He had prepared the way ahead of time so that Will had his Masters degree in counseling.

The Lord's Treat for Naphtali

We were so concerned about our 18-year old daughter Naphtali taking her first flight alone to do her DTS in Australia. She had a 20-hour layover in Kuala Lumpur, Malaysia where she was given a complimentary hotel room before going to Brisbane. The Lord provided her with two Christian Malaysian girls to sit with in the airplane for 15 hours. And then she met a Christian young man in the hotel elevator, who was also going to Brisbane to attend a Bible school. So she was able to see the city of Kuala-Lumpar with a godly young man without being afraid. I could hardly believe it. Oh, yes, I can! Our Heavenly Father can protect and provide so much better for our loved ones. She wrote in her note, "I am praying that, more than all else, I will seek God daily and come back more mature and likened to Christ's example."

Go Hopi Bruins!

There will not be our New Life Ladies Group anymore when there is a Hopi basketball home game, or at the nearby towns 1-3 hours away in Winslow, Tuba City, Gallup, etc. John is playing for the Varsity Team with Hopi High, I realized the importance of showing up for these games not only to support our son, as parents, but I saw that it was not a good testimony to our Hopi friends not to show up for these games.

Besides, we hardly get any showing of the people for any events when it is a game night as these basketball games are so important to the Hopis. So why fight it when we can join it? After all, the Bible says that we need to be "wise as a serpent." So now our New Life Ladies Group got moved to another evening whenever there is a game on Thursday evenings. Will and I holler and scream along with the others, "Yeah, go Hopi Bruins! Go, Hopi, go! Bruins, you can do it!" as loud as we can, as often as we can. It is very

A view from our bedroom window in Hopiland

184

moving to hear so many Hopi friends cheering for our son, John, by name. We feel like they have accepted us as a part of their community.

Instead of Casinos

The Hopi Tribe has just purchased another property in Flagstaff, "Heritage Square." This is the third shopping center that the Hopi Tribe has purchased. Instead of casinos for their people, the Tribe instead invests in other assets. The Hopis believe that they are now in the Fourth World and that the world had been judged and destroyed three times prior by Creator God because of gambling and other impure ways. Will and I believe it is because of their good business sense, and their tenacity to hold on to so much of their ancient ways, that God has a special calling for the Hopi nation. God has called us to a very peculiar and special people.

"We must decide which God we are going to follow"

(From Will) *Millie and I just got home from the jail an hour ago. What a great night! At the end, Millie was praying for a young man who had just received the Lord. He was in tears over accidentally killing a female pedestrian in Shungopavi last week. I'll meet with him tomorrow, Lord willing. He is all torn up over what happened.*

Meanwhile, I was chatting with "Peter" and "Herbert". Peter told me how another fellow here, "Joseph", had gotten down on his knees to receive Jesus through Peter's leading in their cell. Then he and Herbert went on to say that they had asked Juanita, the detention officer, if they could start their own inmates' church meeting on Wednesday nights. And she said yes, if we would write her a letter to confirm our approval. WOW! PRAISE GOD! This is the same Peter who two months ago said, "We have to decide which God we are going to follow."

185

All of a sudden, lots of good stuff is happening. These guys really need prayer for protection, wisdom, etc. We are asking that the gifts start getting imparted powerfully in the Spirit—that we see pastors, teachers, prophets, evangelists, and apostles rising up here. Although just seeing some baptisms would be great, too

Grief Share

There will be a "Grief Share" support group starting at the YWAM facility soon. Each 13-week series will start with a video seminar (approx. 35 minutes), which will deal with the practical issues such as: "When your dreams fall apart, Seasons of grief, Emotions of grief, Your family and grief, Where is God?, Your greatest resource, Stuck in grief or moving on, Growing through grief, God's spiritual hospital and Longing for heaven." We are praying that this would be a place where many Hopi people who have lost their loved ones can come and share their feelings and

know that they are not alone but that God's wonderful comfort and hope is there for them through Christ our Lord.

The "Grief Share" time has been announced in the "Tutuveni" Hopi newspaper. Once again, I see that the Hopi people are somewhat reserved and reluctant to share their grief when there is so much need for healing after the deaths of many loved ones. Or perhaps, it is because there are so many deaths that one could hardly begin to grieve before another loss occurs. I attended two funerals alone only two weeks ago. The Hopi Guidance Center, Director of the veterans program, called wanting us to bring the program to their center; however, we are concerned that this would defeat the opportunity to freely share Christ and to be able to pray for people. We only had one other call and we may need to approach others more personally

To Seek for the things of His mantle

What a beautiful day this is! More people that are dear to us have died recently. And I thank the Lord for the meaning of life. ALL is foolishness...our lack of love, pride, malice, disordered desires, self-absorption, etc. Only I realize how blessed I am when I recognize that it is not how big my house is or how many beautiful things I have, but that I have a loving husband who is still living and breathing, and three terrific kids.

One other thing that the Lord has been speaking into my heart was to ask for the mantle of "Teaching and Intercession." And He spoke in my heart to write to Fern Noble, a native Cree sister with these giftings, and to ask for her mantle. When approached she blessed me fully with her words without holding back.

The Men in orange suits

Will was gone and Terry Wildman could not go into the jail to do ministry Monday night, so I ended up going by myself. I must admit that I was a bit reluctant. And yet, when I saw many of these inmates in their orange suits coming in and filling the dining hall, I knew I was among my brothers and friends. I read out of Ezekiel 2, which the Lord spoke to me prior to coming to Hopiland. "Daughter of man, I am sending you to the Israelites (Hopi, in this case) to a rebellious nation that has rebelled against me; they and their fathers have been in revolt against me to this very day. The people to whom I am sending you are obstinate and stubborn...Do not be afraid of them or their words. Do not be afraid though briars and thorns are all around you and you live among scorpions. You must speak my words to them, whether they listen or fail to listen."

I shared with them that I am not putting them down; with my own heritage as a Korean, I know that my people are also stubborn. We, YWAM, have been coming in these past 4 ½ years to the jail to say to them that God can transform every aspect of their lives and this Hopiland, as they give their lives to honor the Lord and pray for their nation. Many of the inmates came and greeted me with warm greetings and handshakes afterwards, and I knew that the Lord had gone before me. It was so good to spend more than an hour with the lady inmates also. At the end, we stood in a big circle and prayed together for their nation.

"Songs and Tea"

"Songs and Tea" began because when I went to visit my best friend, Ida Walking Bear Murdock, who is 84 years old. One day, I found her at her home utterly beside herself because she had fallen again and had cried. I asked whether she would like to come over to my house. Usually when she comes over she watches a video and sometimes we play a board game, but this time I asked Ida whether she would play the piano so we could sing together. We went through many pages in the hymnal together and sang for about an hour and a half, and found ourselves lifted up in our spirits. So we said we ought to invite other ladies so they could also be encouraged. Ida said she would buy the cookies and I said I would

188

provide the tea. So now we do this once a week at our home in our sun room.

A Passover meal and a Barbecue

We thank the Lord for Marty and Elyse Reitzen, our "Bro Jew" from Santa Barbara, who came and did a "Passover Meal" for us at the YWAM building. It was so precious to have these days of refreshing!

How about "Barbecue hamburgers" for Sunday School? The children all came down to our home this past Sunday and played in the garden, drew pictures, watched the "Prince of Egypt" movie (about Moses) and simply enjoyed being together. I remember how special it was for me to visit my Sunday School teacher's home when I was little. And it was good to simply give them lots of hugs for a lesson because it seems many have heard the Word, but they want to see Jesus in the flesh and how wonderful it is when that can be done through our lives!

Another Baptism

There has been another baptism in Polacca just last week! It is the fourth person in that mesa in the past five years. He was another young man who received the Lord in Hopi Jail. Yes, the Lord is working; His light has come! Only if you knew what kind of a MIRACLE this is for a man to be baptized in Hopiland. It is as though God's power has made a major breakthrough in this land because it means that this man has seen the beauty of the Lord, and is willing to face the persecution he will encounter from now on. We are praying for God's protection.

Praying for the Postmaster

As I entered the post office in Kykotsmovi, I sensed in my heart that the Lord wanted me to ask our Postmaster, Gloria, whether I could pray for her. In the six years that we have been in Hopiland, I had always had a cordial exchange but never a prayer together. In order to ease into asking whether I could pray for her, I asked how her life was going these days. She is a quiet, gentle lady and in her soft voice she asked me whether I remembered her having had a bad back pain awhile back, so much that she could hardly work. She then said to me that Will had asked if he could pray for her and that ever since then, about six months ago, her back was healed. Glory to God! He is making Himself evident in His power to those whom He chooses. And it gave me another opportunity to pray with her again to bless her day.

Bringing the wind rather than the rain

It seems so often that when the dances are being held in Hopiland in the different villages, there have been severe winds. Just recently, an elder told his people that he is not going to join the dances any longer saying that the young men who are supposed to be pure and cause the rain to come are only bringing dust storms because of their wicked deeds. Today, there was a dance in both Shungopovi and Moencopi villages but there was no wind. However, the fire in the east of Arizona is burning out of control, and many of the Hopis are worried. I had calls from two Hopi Christians asking whether I could pray with them yesterday concerning this fire in Arizona. I knew that the Lord had won their hearts when they call a missionary to ask to pray on the phone together.

Anglo youth from Utah

I am thankful for the Jr. High youth group that came out from Park City, Utah for five days this past week. I did not know

190

quite what to think when Kathy, who had been on staff with our Sea & Summit Expeditions over 25 years ago and stayed as our faithful friend all these years, wanted to bring nineteen of their Junior High kids. It turned out that these white youth from an affluent town gave out so much to the Hopi children both in Hotevilla and Kykotsmovi that I was very much impressed! Perhaps, the Hopi kids needed to not only see the Korean youth come, but it is good to have these wonderful experiences with the Anglo youth who are closer to them in age as buddies and friends.

The Morning Glories

Morning glories are growing at Hopi Jail. The ladies in the jail are telling me that some inmates have planted the seeds that I

Morning Glories in five colors: purple, sky blue, white, fuchsia, and pink at our front gated entrance way, in Hopiland.

gave them for Monday night church. It was a lesson about the "Seeds in different soils." How beautiful it would be to see the morning glories blooming in the array of sky blue, pink, white, and purple colors outside on the jail walls. However, once again, I recognize that Hopiland is not a haven for my flowers. In some ways, it is a reminder of the heart state of the Hopi nation. Many of my flowers have died in the heat and the desert wind. And yet, Will and I see small glimpses of hope everywhere with those who are deciding to follow Christ.

As it turns out, these Morning Glories are so hardy that they could survive almost anywhere. They are so hardy and grow at such a rapid rate in some areas that I have heard that some States have made it illegal to grow these flowers.

We had a Ladies' Fellowship at our Condo back in Santa Barbara. I felt that the group was to have the name of a flower. So,

191

we prayed and looked up hundreds of different flowers in a Garden Book to find a name suitable. And we all agreed that the name was to be the "Morning Glories." I didn't know that this group was to be my training ground for coming out to Hopiland, as these twelve beautiful ladies turned out to be so much joy and then, there were some heart breaking moments too.

One of these Morning Glory ladies, Cheryl Murillo, once brought to the group, a whole vine of these flowers which was so entangled and entwined together that we understood why we were to call our group by that name. Like these Morning Glories which come in so many different colors, so our ladies glorify God in their multi hued personalities!

River rafting trip cancelled

My spirit is a bit low today, and we need your prayers. Will's white water river rafting trip with the Hopi youth from the Guidance Center has been cancelled. The Lord had given us an opportunity to join the Korean and Hopi youth to go on a weeklong outing to the Arkansas River in Colorado last year, and it was very successful. The Korean kids sang their praise songs on the river and the Hopi youth loved it and asked more questions concerning the Lord, and testimonies were shared. At a Hopi Guidance Center meeting, a counselor who had joined the trip shared how he had enjoyed the Korean students and their sharing. A red flag went up at the center and they decided to cancel the next river rafting trip as they saw us as "proselytizing" when the Korean youth were simply sharing who they were. We will keep the week open so that the Lord may still allow us to take some of the older Sunday School teens who are no longer coming to church because they have now been initiated in the Hopi ways.

The Lord has been kind to us. Even as I am writing, Will and Naphtali (who is now back from her Discipleship Training School in Australia) are out with Hopi Guidance Center girls doing an expedition. Someone must have been praying, as we were, because the Director changed his mind and decided on a shorter trip (3 days), but with no Korean youth. Naphtali will write soon to tell of her experience in Australia, Malaysia, Egypt, and Ethiopia.

Staying longer than the average missionaries

More pastors in Hopiland have left. The Nutters, from Bacavi Church have left after three years at the end of June. Also, Pastor Arne and Marge Thompson from the Assembly of God church in Polacca have left after being here a little over five years. We had heard that the missionaries long ago had stayed for many years, but when we first arrived, the missionaries, pastors and the Mission School teachers have stayed less than two years. So, all these people have stayed longer than the average missionaries in recent years. There are only seven churches in Hopiland and when one leaves, we can really feel it because we are in close contact with one another.

All is well because He lives!

There are certain things I cannot share about in detail. The pornography, extra marital relationships are rampant here and lesbianism and homosexuality has come into this land. These sins may not be any worse than some of my own sins in my heart; they nevertheless, need repentance and healing for sure. There is God's mercy available.

Did we make much progress? The battle is stronger than ever! These things are normal in the outside world, but when it happens to a nation with a small population, it seems to magnify the evil. We would have left as the others have if we did not know for certain that the Lord has called us here long term to simply love the people with the message of His Great Love. Only if they would know that Jesus can fulfill their deepest needs and desires with His holy love and acceptance and give them peace which this world cannot give!

Will's Trooper made a screeching noise in the engine and had to be towed to our mechanic in Flagstaff in the morning. I was driving our daughter's little car after Will's car was towed away, and was rear ended by a huge truck, the very same afternoon. I am thankful that ALL IS WELL because He lives!

Three Hopi maidens painting at the Watch tower
Once a maiden gets married, she would not wear her hair in a squash blossom
style (right) ever again.
Princess Leah in "Star Wars" got her hair style from Hopi (ha!)

When all seemed dark, the Lord has encouraged us with positive responses from the villages of Tewa, Shipaulovi, Lower Moencopi, and Bacavi, desiring to do trips with us, but now we have no space. We pray that even during the school season the doors would remain open.

Seventh year and no children's worker

As I may have mentioned before, Sundays are the hardest for me. We are going into our seventh year in Hopiland, and I just felt like I had nothing to give, to lead the worship and teach the Sunday School children. "Would you send someone to help with the children, Lord?" It is too hard to teach all the children with ages ranging from 3-14 years. I try to teach the older ones first while having the little ones look at "Veggie Tales" or one of the Bible stories on video first, and then switch, but our solar power was all drained today. The Lord was good though! We sat outside under the shade of the tree and sang, prayed, and learned.

Hopi "Gospel Hour" on the radio station

I was again so amazed to find the "Gospel Hour" on Hopi KUYI (meaning "water") radio station this morning. They played singers like Michael W. Smith, Maranatha singers, and our Mohawk friend, Jonathan Maracle. The song "So Help Me Jesus" by Kris Kristofferson, and "Great Is The Lord" was also played. It was an awesome thing to sit in my kitchen, listening to even African Soul, and Reggae Christian songs lifting up the name of Jesus, in Hopiland. The Lord is working!

Water Fountain Baptisms in Jail

Two young men were baptized tonight in Hopi Jail. These two tough looking young men, one Hopi and one Navajo, among some others tonight had received Jesus into their lives. They were challenged to take the next step to be initiated into walking with Jesus and to stand publicly in baptism. If you were there tonight in Hopi Jail, you would have seen that the Holy Spirit was there as water was poured down their faces from their shaven heads, dripping down to their shoulders, and their eyes closed and their faces in such peace. Afterwards, the two young men introduced themselves to each other and left the room saying that they would come to the men's discipleship group on Saturday night. Once again, there is a waiting list; a maximum of twelve men can come on Saturday night.

A visit only through a thick glass

Our friend "Tyler"(not his real name) who had been so faithful to come to our Jail church services was in there for a serious offense, while driving under the influence of alcohol. He is now far away in prison, so we were able to go see him. However, we were only able to visit him through a thick glass window and with head phones and speakers on the other side. Tyler sounded happy that he is the Chaplain's assistant in the prison.

"Tyler" is a very good writer with a very fine and meticulous hand-writing. He wrote to us regularly from the prison. It made us happy to read that despite the troubles all around him that the Lord's presence and His protection were there with him. In doing ministries, one seldom gets any "thanks" from anyone, but this young man of God wrote saying that if it was not for the Lord's love and the calling for him to be saved that he really would not know how else he would be today. He wrote that he was in the Lord's steadfast love and signed his name.

Another assault

We were violated once again by a young man who had been a part of our family. He came last week and went into a rage, breaking our front metal screen door, throwing things on our deck, breaking our fence. He spat on our 17-year old son, John's face when he was told that he could not come in for he was under the influence of alcohol. This happened when we were not at home. John had to call the police and he was badly shaken when we had spoken to him on the phone. I felt so angry for I felt I could handle almost anything but to see our son at risk of harm by some raging person. And yet, I realized that this raging person was in some ways our son too.

How can we be angry at this young man who was so courageous to make a decision to follow Christ in Hopiland and be our friend? I know that he had suffered for visiting us so much in our home as he was made fun of by other relatives and friends and persecuted by his own family.

I was gone to California to speak to the Korean pastors when his two younger brothers were killed in a car accident. I received a phone call from Naphtali who said that she had just come back from attending their wake. She was choking up on the phone. She said that this young man was going back and forth between the two coffins, gently fixing the lining, around the bodies of his two younger brothers. He used to bring his youngest brother sometimes to our home. He was such a handsome boy, so full of life and looking up to his older brother. He was 11 years old when he died in this car accident. The other brother used to be a rodeo champion. I remember the sadness which had gripped my heart so wrenchingly that I felt like my heart would bleed and I could not stop crying after the phone call.

Lunch hours at Hopi High, reading the Word

John is continuing the KFC (Kids For Christ) group on Wednesdays at Hopi High. He has started, once again, to make all the sandwiches, etc. on Tuesday evenings, for the kids who would come to the Bible Study, so that 45 minutes would not be wasted waiting in line in the cafeteria. But, he felt that was not enough. He said he prayed about it and decided that he should be in Mr. Wirth's room every single day and open his Bible and read during the lunch hour so that anyone can come and study with him and ask questions. In particular, he said he would ask one other Hopi young man named "Buck" to join him, and Buck did.

197

Chapter 18

Desert Roses and Tomatoes

Desert roses, other wild flowers and even tomato plants have come up all on their own in place of all my other flowers that died. It is wonderful when God surprises us with fruit that we didn't expect. I had unintentionally planted the seeds of the cherry tomatoes when I put over ripe ones in the compost last year. Then this year I added the composted mulch into the soil. The result may not be that which we had planned, but according to God's Perfect Plan. It really shows me the power of His Life, and the surprising power of His Spirit working within His Kingdom. We have so much hope.

No option of Baptisms by Emersion

Something wonderful is happening all around us. There have been more baptisms in the jail in Hopiland. Last night, yet another Hopi young man from Polacca, after our Monday night service, came up and was baptized. We don't have the option at this point of "baptism by emersion" in jail, so we just pour ice cold water over their heads from the water fountain, which is there for the inmates in the cafeteria.

Our DTS hiking amongst desert roses

This young man had received the Lord after hearing the salvation message soon after he had tried to commit suicide in the jail last year. He said that he knows, even though many others will say things against him, he needs to choose this path and be baptized!

And on the Saturday discipleship night with the men, two other men (one Hopi from Shongopavi, and another Navajo brother) were baptized. Another recent baptism was a Zuni married to a Hopi.

Finally Hopi men on the San Juan River

Will, after more than six years of being here, was finally able to take Hopi men out on a river rafting trip for three days. Remember Hopiland is high desert. And now, they are almost

Sometimes we get to see much wild life along the river

begging to go more, whereas we could hardly even give these trips away before. We have done many wilderness trips with the youth of all the different villages in Hopiland, but not with the men. I believe God has taken us on another step in this adventure with the men here.

A price worth paying to sleep on the bathroom floor

A beautiful woman (Hopi and Navajo) in her 40's showed up at our door yesterday. She had received the Lord just a month ago and was interested in coming to our New Life Ladies' Fellowship. She was absolutely glowing! She said she almost became a medicine woman and since she has come to Jesus, she is so persecuted by her families that she sometimes sleeps on the bathroom floor. She was in tears as she talked of the Lord's deep love that she sensed in her life. He would sometimes wake her up in the bathroom, in the middle of the night, and ask her to open the Bible and speak into her heart. Her family members have told her that if she truly loved her mother, who recently passed away, she would not choose this new path. We have not seen her again since that visit. Our prayer is that the seed of the resurrection power of Jesus would continue to grow within her, wherever she may be today.

DTS – Yes!

We will be conducting a Discipleship Training School in March 2003 at our YWAM facility in Hopiland. This is a 5 ½ month school which is designed to help people get to know God better, find increased effectiveness in their personal walk with Him and educate them to bring the Good News of Jesus to the peoples of the world – especially the Native American world. The school is both lecture and experiential. More than half of our speakers will be Native Americans themselves. We have much to learn from the tribal host people of this Land. Our two-month outreach will be to the Indian reservations of the Southwest U.S., e.g., Hopi, Navajo and Apache.

A Vivid picture of the enemy's attack

It was a strange night and we were all awakened by noises of dogs running in circles around our home in Kykotsmovi. Will went outside around 2:00 AM to see whether our puppy, "Daisy" was okay. I had heard what sounded like fierce barking, and intense panting of an animal being chased around our house by a whole bunch of other wild animals. Will only found some dog dung right against our back door. When he came back inside, he sensed such a heavy spiritual battle that he began to pray loudly, and John also woke up and joined in with his worship songs on the guitar.

We found our "Daisy" in the morning with parts of her leg gone and meat hanging loose. Our rez veterinarian said she had seen some sheep mauled as badly as this, but not a dog whose muscles and veins were so damaged and literally eaten alive. This was a vivid demonstration of how the enemy wants to devour, kill and destroy us. But, our God is good and gives life.

After six hours of standing to assist with the surgery, at a make-shift clinic in Hard Rock, on the Navajo reservation, Daisy was released to take home. Will and Johnny and I took shifts to nurse her throughout the night. In the morning, having heard her deep sigh, we found our Daisy had died. I am so much more deeply sad than I would have ever imagined! We will not see her bounding and leaping like a deer, to greet us each time we come home. She had been such a joy to Will and our kids. I went out back to sit in my garden and realized that I would not ever see her coming to be near me among the desert flowers again. I never knew that a death of an animal could have such a deep and profound affect on me. I would pay almost any amount to have her come back now.

The enemy has tried to bring harm to our marriage, our kids, and now our animals. Our marriage has not only survived, but a deeper respect for one another has developed. Our kids have thrived with some loneliness, but now our puppy is dead. I thank Jim and Celine Murphy, who come weekly from Flagstaff to pray and do intercession with us, for being with me all yesterday, helping at Dr. Ruby's home/ clinic. I believe the enemy has hit us in every way possible, but God's joy has been much greater than the grief we have suffered.

As we were driving back last night in the dark, with Daisy in the back of the car with me, we praised and worshiped our Lord in songs for He is still worthy! And I told the Lord that I would worship and honor Him no matter the outcome. Yes, our Lord is still the champion. I think I will see Daisy wagging her tail and coming to greet me in Heaven someday. Yes, I believe that the Lord may just have many surprises in heaven.

Baptism - a final betrayal of Hopi

Will had gone to visit a young man, and they took a long walk together on top of the mesa. This young man told Will that he had shared with his uncle that he had been baptized in jail. The uncles play a very important role in Hopiland. His uncle told him that he was, *ka Hopi*, no longer a Hopi, and that he would not be able to participate in any of their ceremonies.

Because of their historical experience with the church, Hopis see baptism as the final point of betrayal of the Hopi ways which encompass all aspects of their lives. They were told in the past, once they became a Christian that they could not go to any of the dances in the plazas, including the Social dances, nor any other events. This meant that they could no longer be Hopi. This young man told Will that he prayed about what his uncle had said, and that the Lord told him that he could continue to go to the kiva if he would read his Bible and obey His Spirit.

Syncretism versus Critical Contextualization

I believe that this is a sad thing that the enemy of our soul would love to confuse and cut off these Hopi believers from their families and their community, because of the church's failure to bring the truths of scripture into the context of the people's culture. Understanding the distinction between what is "syncretism" versus "critical contextualization" is crucial for those bringing the Gospel into another culture. According to our friend, Art Everett,

Syncretism is the blending together of incompatible unbiblical religious beliefs with Biblical Christian faith – a true

The Hopis are dry Farmers, so they do not do any irrigation. Hopi corn and beans and melons are grown out in the field or in their family terrace garden plots. Their seeds have been cultivated for many generations to grow in the high dry desert. The Hopis use their planting stick to dig deep into the sand to throw their seeds in. Their dances on the mesas are prayers to bring down the rain. Long ago, before all the stores, automobiles and highways, people could die of starvation if they didn't have a good harvest. The basket is woven from Yucca plant which is harvested and often colored to make designs.

Christian cannot accept syncretism. Critical Contextualization, on the other hand, would still allow faithfulness to the integrity and testimony of Scripture in a new cultural situation because there is no universal way to communicate the Gospel that is understood equally well in every culture. This requires finding unique ways to present the Gospel in every setting to every people. The Gospel would be shared in the Context of the people group rather than trying to present a totally new culture.

By cutting off these young believers from their society, it also cuts them off from being a witness to their family members. What will happen to these people? Would they survive all the scrutiny and the persecutions from their own people and even from the Hopi church? Or would they be discouraged and go back to their old ways?

Should we not baptize at all? No, we believe that this was the Lord's command and that this is the time to baptize all those who ask. Even for those short moments of faith, to be able to stand before the others to say that "Jesus, indeed, is the Lord" is doing something huge in the heavenlies. Oh, how we desperately need prayer in this new season. Pray for the strength of these new ones who are being baptized and for them to dare to stand firm once they are out of jail, and not to abandon the love of Christ, but to grow to spread the Gospel.

Wedding Bells

Wedding bells, white streamers and balloons were hung around our house. It was a privilege to host Jon and Marcia Eckstrom, and to host their reception after the wedding in Ohio. Jon was the man who we first visited seven years ago when we found out that the Lord was calling us to Hopiland. He and his late wife, Molly, from Wycliffe Bible translators, were the ones in the span of 20 years who translated the New Testament into the Hopi language. They paid a heavy price to be able to do this, as they had to move many times from one village to another, as they were quietly resisted. Now, the Lord put Jon together with Marcia Neher, who had been praying for Hopi for over 30 years.

"Asna"- Hair washing

During their stay in our home this week, Jon talked about how it may be more appropriate in Hopiland to do sprinkling of the water for baptism than immersion, because it is the Hopi way into every stage of initiation: into life and marriage and death. Every Hopi goes through what is termed "Asna," head wash, as a baby. During a wedding a man and his bride's hair are washed, "Kuuyit," meaning mark with water. And finally, when they are buried. The word Messiah in Hopi is "Mong'asi'taqa" meaning Head-wash Chief. Do we continue in their cultural way to "mark with water" by head washing or do we immerse? From our point of view this is a contextual question. If the Hopis were considering this they would be self theologizing. May the Lord give us all wisdom!

Native Songs and dances at the NAWR

I believe it is the first time that the Hopi ladies have been invited to do something special during the Northern Arizona Women's Retreat in Flagstaff. We will be singing "Were you there when they crucified my Lord?" and "As the Deer" in Hopi, accompanied by a beautiful Native American flute music CD. I was curious as to why there was no verse in the Hopi hymnal which said, "Were you there when He rose up from the dead?" The Hopis believe that when they die, they go back down into their underworld, but as those who believe in the power of resurrection, we should beg to differ. The last verse, therefore, was quickly made up in Hopi. And, Daryla, a Navajo Christian sister, had gladly agreed to come and do her beautiful dance while the Hopi ladies sang in front of about 350 other women. This was a beautiful picture of reconciliation between the two tribes which were at enmity against each other at one time.

When we were done and I had looked up at the crowd after helping the older ladies off the stage, I saw that all 350 ladies were up, giving their standing ovation. I knew that the standing ovation was not for us, but unto the Lord! They had sensed an excitement in their spirit, as we had already sensed, that the Lord of the Universe was doing an awesome new thing amongst the Native Americans and that they were now the evangelists to go out to the ends of the earth, as Dr. Billy Graham had spoken in the early 1970's saying, a "sleeping giant is about to awaken and they are the original people of this land, the Native Americans. And they will be our next evangelists."

Not a quiet life

When we first came to Hopiland, I thought that we would have a quiet life out here in the middle of the high desert. We've had so many people come through our home in the past few weeks that it would spin one's head. I am glad that one of the things I enjoy most in my life is "hospitality." I could be sick like a dog and yet when we have company, I could serve tea and dessert. Thank you, Bill Gowey, for bringing Jonathan Maracle's powerful music to Hopiland! It is another step to further God's power to free His people!

Not a quiet life until we are on our river rafting trip

Chapter 19

Seeing More Than Twelve Coyotes

In some Native American cultures, certain beliefs are so strong that one cannot blow it off too easily. One of these beliefs is that when someone sees a coyote crossing the path in front of them, that it is a sure sign of death for that person or to one of their loved ones. I had heard that some Navajos will stop their cars and turn around if they see a coyote on their path. It has been almost uncanny that I have counted more than a dozen coyotes crossing in front of our cars this year alone. It seems almost impossible that they should be right in our path at just the right moment, on that stretch of 200 miles, round trip into Flagstaff and back. Some of these coyotes were so close that I could see their eyes looking back at me and then darting off. I have talked to one Hopi Christian woman and she simply told me, "Someone is putting curses on you, but they can't touch you because our God is greater!"

A House in Flagstaff

In 1998, after two years of being in Hopiland, we were told that we could no longer rent out our little condo in Santa Barbara as it was the rule of the County moderate income housing program. And so, we sold that condo and bought a house in Flagstaff. I cried for three days as I washed the dishes and did other things around the house and in our office. I thought it would be our retirement home someday. I believe now that the Lord wanted me not to look back, and to sever any thinking that I had a home back in Santa Barbara. My home is now with the Hopi people in Hopiland.

Does a missionary have to be poor?

I believe that God wants us to be wise for all His kingdom purposes. We don't want to be on welfare in our old age, but rather be able to give to other ministries, many ministries.

Will looked at me just before falling asleep in bed and told me that we don't have anything saved up for our retirement, and that we needed to do something more. Most people working for firms or for government agencies have help with paying into Social Security and some type of a retirement plan.

I remember a time when we couldn't even afford a tin roof house. Once, we looked at a house in the town of Ojai, about 35 miles inland from Santa Barbara. When we first married our $600 a month salary as the Directors of a ministry was dirt poor, even in the early eighties. And, we had to pay $150 rent to the ministry. Now we were making more, but still it was a miracle that a realtor gave us even the time of day.

The Realtor lady showed us a "Quonset hut" home down near the bottom of a dry river bed, below a dam. It was actually pretty nice inside. When I saw the army barracks tin house, I could not believe that this was my lot in life, but at $40,000 it was much more than we could afford. Afterwards, Will and I took our little baby daughter, Clover, to the McDonald's for lunch and comforted ourselves. I remember my elephant tears dropping into my hamburger that day as Will quietly rubbed my back.

The Lord was gracious and it was amazing to see how He has provided a way for us to secure an investment for the future for us.

I feel that sometimes, if a missionary has done well with their finances that they get punished by not being supported by some churches. If any lay people could invest and give an inheritance to their children, the missionaries should also be able to do this without being judged. And I have seen also those who had squandered their finances and have not been wise and have nothing, made out to be the heroes as missionaries. It's as though those who don't have much are so much more spiritual and holy. Things are not always what they seem.

"What a Wonderful World"

Our family was treated to a night of "Amahl and the Night Visitors" play and symphony at NAU (Northern Arizona University) by our daughter Clover. The play in the opera form was simply beautiful! On the second half of the program was the Flagstaff Symphony with a parade of Christmas songs in honor of our Savior. It was a display of marvelous costumes and programs. When over 300 school children went up and sang, "What a wonderful World," I found my eyes fill with tears for I knew that as painful as this world can be, there is such beauty in this world. May His beauty and the presence of our magnificent King reside in you all throughout this Christmas season!

The best part of our Christmas was when our daughters, Clover and Naphtali were resting on the couch next to me so that I could run my fingers through their hair. We were in the warmth, by our wood and coal burning stove in our living room. And, together, we watched a movie, "A man called Peter," by Catherine Marshall. All the Christmas music has now stopped playing and the girls have gone back to University and our home in Flagstaff. Will and John are also gone on a rock climbing trip with two Hopi boys. How blessed I am when there are noises and messes to clean up because there are loved ones who came. One must not complain about these things, for where there is any beauty to be had, most likely there are some noises and some messes.

"Will not go down into the kivas anymore"

A museum kiva in Utah.

One of these young Hopi men told us that he went down into the kiva to pray after much urging from his mother to do so. December is the quiet month when there is no drumming and when men go down to pray and fast. However, he told us that he had a terrible experience with pain in his knees, as though there was a burning fire and many needles. He even went to a medicine man who told him that someone had gathered his spit from the ground and cursed him. This Hopi brother told his mother that he is not going down to the kiva anymore to pray with these men.

A whole year of Fasting

A whole year of fasting from thrift shopping, antique shopping, and yard sales has already come to an end for me. At the beginning of this year, the Lord had spoken to my heart not to go to any of these places, including even to other Department stores, but only go shopping for food and necessities. As one with artistic leanings, I have loved these Thrift shops because I think what they sell is much more creative and unusual, as I find most of the Department stores and the Shopping Malls to be so typical and boring. At first, I went through some withdrawal symptoms when I would go by big yard sales or thrift shops. It is not that I believe everyone needs to do this. Our Father does mind, however, when this becomes a bondage and a false comfort. He loves us and cares so much. I do believe that He is asking of us to listen to His small voice and to give Him the very gift of obedience.

Red clay potteries are often painted with yucca needles and baked in dried sheep dung outside.

Chapter 20

No More "Feeling Like a Beggar"

Our son John had torn a ligament on his knee while playing basketball at Hopi High. We were told that if we did not get the surgery done while he is still young that this can turn into arthritis later.

Our son John's surgery was done yesterday, as scheduled. John is now equipped with drainage tubes, built-in circulation ice tube to prevent swelling, a cast and crutches! Now, if that doesn't make him feel loved and cared for, I don't know what would. I am very grateful for our personal intercessor, Celine, who insisted that I let the need of healing for John's knee be made known. And I am also grateful that one of our friends wrote desiring to help with the surgery fund, saying, "We have not because we ask not." Will also had surgery done the same morning on his "trigger finger" thumb. It was a father-son surgery, done by one doctor together in the same room.

I believe the surgery was the healing which our son, John, needed physically, emotionally, and spiritually. He needed to know that his personal needs would be met as a missionary child. This need goes back generations in my family. My father told me that he hated being a "preacher's kid" growing up, back in Korea, before the war. As a musical Child Prodigy, he could not attend a very prominent Music Academy even when he was recruited, because my grandparents were so poor. My grandfather served in the ministry for over 65 years of his life, later becoming the head of a major denomination in Korea. Even still, there was much sadness when my father said, "I always felt like a beggar as a child."

I thought I had heard a similar voice in John when we had first told him we would need to postpone his knee surgery for a lack of finances. That was almost more than I could bear. I felt I could almost endure anything, but to see another generation think as my father did, feeling like a beggar, was unbearable. I truly believe that John's love for God would not have allowed him to be bitter, and yet I am so grateful that the Lord provided in this way.

John as a little boy, playing "Indians" with his buddy, Eric

It does not help sometimes that the Body of Christ makes one feel like a beggar. When we were serving in Missions back in California, I had talked to a woman at our Church about her couch which was announced in the Church bulletin to be given away. I called and asked, "Oh, by the way, would you tell me the colors and the description of your couch?" She knew that we were missionaries there in the City. I heard a brief silence on the other side of the line. And then, she said very coldly, "You know, beggars can't be choosy."

Let the tears flow

Will must have sensed that I needed a loving embrace as I sat on the couch. As he held me and gave me a kiss on my face, all I could do was to let my tears flow. I didn't even know what was wrong. I had a dozen ladies show up at our home just the evening before for our New Life Ladies Group which is more than I could

Beautiful Cathedral rocks continue around the bend. We are walking the trail along the side of the San Juan River where the Hopis walked long ago.

have hoped for. We're starting a series called "Healing the Angry Heart," an eight part series through videos. We talk and pray and cry together afterwards and it is so very good. And yet, I find myself almost in a slight depression the last couple of days.

The Scripture teaches us to "hope" in all things. There is a silent language between the missionaries. No one has to talk, and yet one can see the sadness in the others' eyes for we all have seen too many tragedies on the reservation. Would any of these ladies continue to walk in the Lord even a year from now? Do I dare to hope about anything? There have been so much set-backs and disappointments. It often feels as though Satan is winning more than God. Just when we had thought we had seen another stage of our Lord at work here, the enemy moves back in with a full vengeance.

The other day, we took our Hopi brother and his mother and his little nephew to see his brother in the ICU room at the Flagstaff Hospital. The whole time while driving there, the little nephew coughed away. So, I suppose I could have gotten sick from him. I have lost a very good friend who had to move away, partly to be able to find a job in the city, but also to escape the persecutions of being a Christian in her village. There have been more deaths recently. A boy's father was killed in a car accident; a boy whom I taught at Hopi Mission School. This boy was one of my best Art students, and he and his father had joined Will on a Sea & Summit outing. And now he is fatherless. A Hopi sister of mine also lost her son. She had already seen her husband and her other son brought to her front door in a coffin before. Her sorrow is like deep crying out to deep.

The Lord has a way of working out things for GOOD even with three sleepless nights! While Will and John went away after Christmas and I was alone, the young man, whom we have been involved with for the past six years, called. When he is in a drunken state, one cannot predict what can happen. After a scary conversation, I was able to ask one of the ladies in our New Life Fellowship to come and spend the night in the guest room, and I believe we became closer for it. When I had yet another unpleasant phone call the next evening, close to midnight, I was able to call my good friend and her husband, who is the Governor of Kykotsmovi, and they both came and spent the night. On the third night, I invited my Sunday School children to come and we had a wonderful slumber party!

A Painting by a Hopi artist at Grand Canyon watch tower

A Dance, pure in one village, but not the other

As I stood on top of the roof of the Hopi houses watching the Buffalo and Deer Dancers and the Hopi maidens moving to the drum beat of the men singers below on the ground, in the plaza, I felt as though I was in a far away land, in Tibet or some place. My heart cried out for wisdom and I found myself moved to tears as I watched the dance at one village, which seemed pure and lovely, but the other village the next weekend, disturbing. The one I felt disturbed in my spirit about, seemed like it brought such a bad wind storm that it filled our church with dust and sand.

Havasupai- the Blue water people (from Will)

Let me give you a quick glimpse into our unusual world here. I took three Hopi guys down to the Havasupai (Blue Water People)

Rez. Actually, they took me into this amazing deep canyon land with blue/green waterfalls that drain into the Grand Canyon's Colorado River. We ended up staying with a non-believer and his wife, an elder. Several times my Hopi friends were challenged with offers of drugs and/or alcohol, or other ways to compromise, but they stood firm in ways that I don't think were just to impress me.

The hike down descends a few thousand feet over the course of about six miles. We arrived very weary after dark and ended up camping in the bushes off the main trail. The next morning, after breakfast, we worshipped our Lord, read Scripture, and discussed the holiness that He is leading us into. Before and during that time, we had several visitors who greeted us, gave us directions and water, and eventually a yard to camp in. "Dante" and "Gwen" were very generous in the midst of their material scarcity. Dante is a fairly worldly chain smoker, and Gwen, a village elder, is a shy basket maker. Dante, most generously took time on Saturday to give us a tour of the village and the world famous water falls.

Mooney Falls was nearly overwhelming. It is over two hundred feet tall, its power was breathtaking. When Dante led John and I down the rock wall to the pool at the base of the falls, we quickly stripped down, suited up and waded out into what for both of us felt like the living column of God's holy power and majesty. We sang, whooped and hollered in delight as we were blown back by the rushing vapor and powerful water current thrusting us humbly away.

That evening and the following morning, we met with several visitors, including another elder who showed Dante the proper way to sing one of the Havasupai drum songs. Later, at the small Supai Church, we were warmly received, even as Dante was horse packing our backpacks back up to the car on the canyon rim.

This was a special retreat for the guys and me. We did church in the bushes and saw God at work repeatedly. It is our hope and prayer that all these men and women we work with will walk that Jesus path in ways that truly honor Him, and retain their God-given native identities.

He has shown Himself faithful

*Our DTS students working to
prepare Hopi foods during the lecture phase*

The Lord has provided wonderful DTS speakers, and because we have had an "open door policy," Hopi men and women, often join our classes. This would not have been possible when we first came. It is a small beginning, but it is GOOD! Glory to you, Lord! It was so good to have Marvin Yoyokie, the Governor of our Kykotsmovi village, come and welcome the students and staff on the first evening of our school. We are truly thankful to the Lord that He has shown us His faithfulness every step of the way. It was only fitting that, Jon Lansa, a Hopi brother was to be our first speaker. He is presently with the Navigators and taught on "Feeding one's heart through the Word, Bible Study."

Jonathan Eckstrom (Wycliffe Bible Translator, who had translated the New Testament into Hopi language) came with his wife, Marcia, and shared their experiences of their love for the Hopi nation. Mark and Donna MacGowan (Directors of YWAM Denver's Eagle Rock, Colorado base) spoke on the subject of "Fear of the Lord" and led worship for our school.

We are seeing that, as we have opened up our speakers to the public, many Hopis have already come and benefited from the worship time and the topics that are being spoken, and the fellowship. We see that our Hopi brothers and sisters are "event-oriented," and they are coming where the "happenings" are.

Will and I found this school to be more effective than we had expected. We did not, however, have a full understanding of what kind of an extra load, even a small school like this would bring on top of all our staff meetings, staff-student meetings, as well as attending classes and still trying to make home visits, and do existing ministries in the Hopi Jail, etc. I stood and almost burst out crying at one point when I looked out on Sunday morning and saw Charity, our new staff person, and two of our students, Lory and Nick, all helping out with the stories, arts & crafts, and music, snacks, etc. with the children. Thank you so much, Lord, for bringing in the workers!

A Hopi brother in DTS

Our Hopi brother, who is in our school, is an inspiration to all of us. He is the one whom we took out to a Christian rehab program in California and who was kicked out for refusing to cut his long hair. He is doing well now. With him coming to our Discipleship School, here on the reservation, he is saying to all of his family and friends that it is okay for him to be a Hopi and follow Christ. He is helping us make a "Father Drum" which can be played by several people; we will be able to use it for our "Praise & Worship."

Our friend has gone down to the dry wash to pick up some sticks and, with leather, has begun to make drum sticks. A drum beat is like the heart beat of Creator to the Native people. It was not something I liked at first and then, eventually, I realized my heart beat quickening and quietly leaping when I would hear the drum sound. Yes, we can worship Jesus with a Native American drum, even though it does not have the word "Yamaha" written on it. To take away the drums from the Native Christians would be once again calling them a "savage people" and cutting their hair all over again. Sometimes, I think we still want every nation to act like sedate pioneers with organs and hymnals. There is nothing wrong with that, except when one demands all nations to look the same.

Hopi men teaching in jail

Tonight's jail ministry was historical! We have never had two Hopi Christian men preaching the Word there until tonight! Gillie, who was back temporarily from Teen Challenge, and Eddie, from our school, took turns sharing, teaching and praying for the inmates. Randy Woodley shared his Cherokee prayer song with his hand drum and told the men that the Bible was written by brown skinned tribal people, the Hebrews.

Fresh new Hope and Visions

It was also amazing to have the two brothers who were convicted for breaking into our home last year come up to me after the service and sincerely ask me for forgiveness for what they had done. The Hopi Tribe charged them, convicted them and brought them to justice, and we did not even know who they were. Yet, the Lord brought them to the service in Hopi Jail tonight so that they may receive forgiveness and someday know Christ. Later, one of these brothers came to know the Lord and he became our good friend.

We were so grateful that the Lord led Will to drive to Winslow to a pawn shop and found my twelve string Applause guitar hanging in the store. Later, it was the Hopi policeman who went and got it out and brought it back to Hopiland. I wonder what other reservation would go through so much trouble for someone to retrieve a guitar for an outsider, making more than a three hour round trip. Thank you, Lord. Thank you Hopi police!

Our home and YWAM school continues to grow in numbers. We are truly seeing God at work. It is as though there is a burst of energy happening with other Hopis and other guests from other Native nations joining us for the different sessions. It is as though God is freshly giving us a hope and a vision of how future Discipleship Training Schools will have a place in this land. We presently have Randy Woodley (our Cherokee speaker), and his friend Charles from Tennessee, and a family of three, Fern Cloud, plus Rainy and Seth from Minnesota, in our home.

It seemed that we were hardly going to get any Sunday School children on Easter Sunday. After much preparation, this was sad for us. There was the 1st Annual 3K run and an Easter egg hunt in the village of Hotevilla. Then, as we prayed, the Lord spoke in our hearts saying that we should go to the community and ask whether we can help rather than having our own activities at the Church. That is when the community leader said to me, "You can come only if you bring your guitar." So that is how we got to stand in front of the whole Hotevilla community to sing to them the songs of our risen Lord, and have a cookout with them, rather than just having an ordinary service of our own. And they have asked that we work with them every year from now on.

Dancing to a different drum beat

We are seeing more of the younger Hopis coming into different meetings, whereas this was almost impossible to see when we first came here seven years ago. One of the ladies from our New

Life group just got baptized yesterday. These ladies do not believe that they should sing and dress and act like the white man. They

respect the few surviving elders in the churches, but feel that there is anger and judgment against the new generation who may dance to a different drum beat. The Hopis have more of their traditions and ceremonies intact than any of the other tribes in North America, and it is no wonder that they want to keep their identity in their distinct Native expressions, even if one becomes a Christian.

We have been warned

We have had much sickness amongst the students and the staff. We have been warned by a Hopi Christian that someone does not want our Discipleship Training School to happen. When I asked, "Do you mean that they are praying against us?" we were told, "Yes, and not only that, they want us hurt." And yet, we see that every time we've come against sicknesses, attitude problems, despair, that we have had victories each and every time. There is more unity, peace, and respect for one another than ever! Our Lord is more powerful! Our staff, students and the guests are all involved in various ways with Monday jail ministry, men's Talking Circle, Wednesday night open circle, Thursday night New Life Ladies' group, Video Nights at Hotevilla Church, and Sunday Schools.

Although my spirit is encouraged beyond words because I sense that we are at another stage with the people coming to the Lord in Hopiland, I am very tired. This school, although small, has taken a toll on us and there seems to be not enough time between our family, ministries, chores, the office, and administration work, etc. But, oh how the Lord has given us even bigger visions ahead which we cannot even yet see! What a wondrous thing He has done when He has created us and has put His GLORY in us to love and serve Him. At present, we have one of the inmates out of Hopi Jail staying at our home and a potential staff person from Sweden visiting. May the Lord's glory be shown in you and me! God bless you!

Sparrow Water Fountain for my Desert Garden

There is a little fountain in my garden which my friend, Susan, gave me several years ago. She wrote one day saying she felt that the Lord had told her to give me a fountain. Before that, I had only seen her once in ten years. It is a small fountain with three sparrows on top; it sounds just like a small brook! The Lord must have known my life-time desire to have a house near a brook. I turn it on every spring and now a hummingbird (I call it "Bathsheba") comes and drinks and takes her bath in it. Many Irises have bloomed, spreading their green leaves all over my brown desert garden, and Snapdragons and Dianthus flowers have come back with their full array of delightful colors. And now I can sit under my apple tree, which is my place of serenity to draw near to the Lord every morning. It is, indeed, the land of the living!

Co-Valedictorian

Our son, John William, spoke at Hopi High School graduation as the co-valedictorian, at the outside football stadium. Will and I realized that both Naphtali and now John were able to give their testimonies of their love for Christ to one of the biggest crowds ever to be held in Hopiland, both speaking at their graduations. What was even more amazing is that hundreds of hands clapped and applauded, with cheers, when John was giving honor to Jesus Christ in the middle of his speech. John had to pause for the applause to stop in order to continue his speech. The Hopis are a very polite people and they would not have booed John, however, they did not have to give him such a big applause either.

A Beautiful Healing

We were able to watch one of the most beautiful healings take place in one of our Hopi sisters, Nita (Annetta) recently. We were invited to come to a Missions Conference at Mountain Life Evangelical Free church in Utah. So, we took two of our very good Hopi friends and their daughters and one toddler son. All of them looked so radiant in their Hopi regalia. They did their beautiful Basket Dance song in their Hopi language; this traditional song was teaching the children, men and women to live a good life. They also did the motions to a Native American song called "the Birth," by Tom Bee. Afterwards, they both gave their testimonies. A poem which was written by the younger Hopi lady told a story of sexual abuse in her childhood which went on for many years and how death had called out to her over and over again.

The poem also told of how she was raped later in her life, and death called out to her again. But, she told of a man who came and gave her life and that His name was Jesus. She shared how she could not bear to look at the baby that was born as a result of the rape, and gave the baby girl up for adoption. Her tears were coming down her face, and we saw a girl, around nine years old, go up and stand next to her on the stage in front of the church. This girl and the family had come to visit our friends as they lived in Utah and heard that we were not far from their city.

This girl gently wiped the tears repeatedly from our Hopi sister's face. It was then, we heard our Hopi sister say, "And this is the child I could not bear to look at, but all I can see now is the love of Christ" The very one who was the product of a rape was wiping the tears off the one who was her birth mother! The keynote speaker, who speaks all over the world, said it was the most powerful thing he had ever seen at a Missions Conference. Thank you, Lord! You are doing such beautiful things.

A Child is Born

I was a child who knew not what lie ahead
who knew nothing about child abuse
Who couldn't think a father could be the abuser
But, when it came, I wish I was dead
I was a teen who didn't know that
she needed or which way to go
All she could do was to feed it with anger,
hatred, drugs, alcohol and sex.
Still, I wish I was dead
As a young mom, all I could think about was
what that child needed.
And, that was LOVE that I needed
Though this child is without a father
All the mother could say was" Why bother?"
I grew up without a father! Fathers are no good
Still, I wish I was dead.

Yet, another child was born
Only God knew the pain, shame and anger that grew within
"Why me?" was the question to rape
As a young adult with a call of death and no sense of
real love or the strength to go on
There was a man who showed me what I thought was real love
A man who cared, but was not strong enough
to deal with a hurting child, who yet had another child, so he left
Death called more and more

Until I met a man who had a Son who showed me real love
Gave me peace, took my shame, anger, and hatred
He listened to the crying child, helped the teen with anger
Took the pain from the mother,

and showed her LOVE instead of death.
A call of life is now born!
This man is faithful and someone I can trust.
His name is Jesus!

Annetta Lynn Koruh

Korean drums, Bead classes Etc.

IMI Korea and Inter-Varsity teams are both here in Hopiland. They are presenting Korean drums, and songs with a Korean gong to protocol the Hopi elders. Also, Bead classes will be held for three days at YWAM with Linda. This class will be open to the community twice a week at the YWAM facility so that the women in Hopiland can have a skill for a cottage industry.

We believe that one of the purposes as a YWAM base here in Northern Arizona is to partner and to assist the "Church" outside Hopi to catch the vision "to know God and to make Him known." We cannot assist all the churches, and all who call us, but we have partnered with several churches with a long-term commitment to work together in reaching the Hopi nation and beyond.

Will and the male DTS students are going down to Parker, Arizona. This is to take a young friend out of Hopi Jail back to his home. DTS will leave to do "Cleansing Stream" in Texas, and then to outreach in Jemez pueblo reservation in New Mexico.

Dan Vanelli from SIU (Scriptures in Use) will also be here to teach at our School. YWAM Sea & Summit interns from Bishop will be here to work and there is a trip to Jack's Canyon, near Winslow, with the Hopi men planned.

Wearing Mantas at YWAM Hopi

After seven long years, we were able, finally to see two Hopi ladies dare to wear their "mantas," the Hopi dress, and sing and do a motion to a song at our YWAM facility in Hopiland. It is unbelievable that some believe that as a Christian, they cannot even wear their own dress. The dress is not evil in itself. We believe this was another breakthrough in the heavenlies as Satan has tried to keep the Hopi Christians believing that they had to leave all their culture behind and do only as the white people do. Only twice, we were able to see the Hopi ladies wearing the manta in a Christian setting recently, but only outside and never in Hopiland. It may be hard to imagine, but this was likely the first time that this was done in many decades, or maybe ever. It was beautiful to watch them! Glory and honor to our Lord Jesus!

I would now like to compare wearing Hopi Manta to what Jesus said to his disciples concerning eating with unclean hands.

Do you not yet understand that whatever
enters the mouth (what you wear)
goes into the stomach and is eliminated?
(goes on your body and taken off to wash?)
But those things which proceed out of the mouth
comes from the heart, and they defile man.
For out of the heart proceed evil thoughts, murders,
adulteries, fornications, thefts, false witness, blasphemies.
These are things which defile a man ,
but to eat (or to wear a Manta) with unwashed hands
does not defile a man!
(Matthew 15: 17-20)

229

Chapter 21

We Will Rise on Eagle's Wings

I am very blessed. All that I had desired for my life, I found in Jesus, and He has given me more than life abundant. He has brought me to a spacious place and the color brown has become more beautiful to me than ever. I found myself on the ground at my front porch the other week, hanging onto the door knob after having fainted, but life is still good because I know I am blessed for knowing that this is the land of promise!

Tonight, we have our Discipleship Training School graduation at YWAM. We thank our Lord for the completion of this school. We will have a good dinner and have guests from other states coming. Nita, our Hopi friend, decorated the YWAM place with many streamers and balloons. There will be a reception following the graduation. We have Polynesian barbeque at our home and we thank Paul Otoko, who is bringing 17 of his

Polynesian family members to serve the Hopi people! Many Hopis and others will come and praise our Lord in our garden.

We are truly thankful that the Lord sent Charity McDonald on staff to help us these past six months with DTS, and now making a longer commitment to stay in Hopiland. She has been a tremendous help with the Children's Ministry in Hotevilla. She has a real passion to reach the children and they love her. She lived in Liverpool, England for two years prior to coming here and worked with the YWAM ministry there.

We are so grateful for all those who went before us to bring the Good News to this land, for they all paid a heavy price. And we are so ever thankful for all those around the world who are praying for a revival in Hopiland; and, for all those who have come to this land to join in our efforts thus far, for this is certainly not about us at all, but God doing a special work at such a time as this! Pray, pray that we may know what the next step is to not lose the momentum. Before coming to Hopiland, in a dream, 10,000 Native Americans had come to know the Lord!

We now have an After-school Hotevilla Girl's Club every Wednesdays and Kykotsmovi Girl's Club is held at YWAM building every Thursdays with Charity McDonald, our new staff person, and she is doing a great job! We were also so excited that some older boys who never come to church anymore after their initiations into the kiva came last night to our Video Night at Hotevilla Gospel Church.

We were thrilled to find out that the KFC (Kids for Christ) Bible study group which Naphtali started four years ago still continues at Hopi High School. In fact, we were concerned that after Naphtali graduated that no one would take the leadership to continue, but then our son John with great fear and trembling, took the leadership and continued the group for two more years until he graduated.

And this year, there are more Hopi High kids attending KFC. We thank Mr. Wirth, who buys and has the pizzas brought in every week from a Hopi Deli as no one wants to prepare sandwiches and snacks and bring them to school. John meets with other Hopi young men outside to keep each other accountable in different areas of sin.

Will and I have been gone for a couple of weeks traveling, resting, and attending DTS Leadership Class at YWAM Montana Lakeside. Now I am more eager than ever to raise disciples all over the world! Even without me, our New Life Ladies Group went on and I am thrilled that they did quite well for this was what I had been praying for these past seven years. Thank you, Father!

We're also being invited to come and speak to a Christian Boarding School in Showlow, Kindergarten - 7th Grade. At first, we were hesitant because we didn't want to be too spread out doing too many things. And then, we realized that the Lord was now giving us an opportunity to speak to a younger generation of Navajo and Apache children. How surprised they may be to see Hopi ladies and children dressed in their own traditional outfits dancing for the Lord! If we could let them see that the Lord is in this kind of expression, they may grow up free to express who they are as the Natives, and love the Lord.

The "Island Breeze" Team

There were over 400 people to watch the "Island Breeze" YWAM team at the Hopi Civic Center this time. Not one person walked out when the presentation of the Gospel was clearly given. We are talking about hundreds of traditional Hopis who showed up after knowing that this was a Christian event. There was a spiritual hunger like we had never seen before. We gave out Bibles afterwards, and some even came up begging for one on their own. Others came up for prayers.

We did not buy enough hotdogs and chips and drinks for this many people for we only had a few days to put out the flyers. And yet, when the last person had finally gotten their meals, we saw that everyone was fed and a few kids had even come up and received second servings. I had only purchased enough for 250 people for we had no idea how many would show up, but we got to see the food multiply as in Jesus' days with the fishes and the loaves.

Our home was filled with the Island Breeze team (all 17 of them) afterwards, and so many others so that we could hardly move. This is somewhat normal. As some of the Hopi ladies were cooking to feed the Island team, other Hopi friends broke out singing hymns like "How great Thou Art" and many more songs in our living room. It was as though they could hardly contain themselves because of the joy they felt in their hearts.

Dying to Self

Since I have been in this land, I felt as though I had to die to myself a thousand times over. I read somewhere that it is doubtful that God could use anyone greatly until one has been wounded deeply. I am sure that it was not the intent of the one who said this to make it sound like our God is a sadistic God, and yet it comforts me to think that perhaps I may be useful to comfort others. However, we should never blame God for what Satan did to us or what we, ourselves may have done to ourselves. Our God has done all that is necessary for us to be loved by Him, and provided all that is needed to have His favor and goodness in my life.

A very famous Apache chief, Geronimo, is reported to have once said, "It is a good day to die." Then, I thought to myself that it is good to die, everyday! It is a good day to die to "self" that is! (Romans 6) I shared this with some of my friends and wrote this in our prayer letter. Next thing, I knew, I saw this in a book and heard it repeated many times by some others. I suppose the others also had the same revelation from what Geronimo said. Besides, nothing on this earth is new under the sun, as it is said in Ecclesiastes.

You would not believe the amount of insecurities and condemnation I feel sometimes in my heart. I don't feel I am worthy to speak in front of a big group and fear that I would desire the glory for myself, but the Lord let me know that He has used even Balaam's donkey and that He wouldn't be pleased if I let go of the opportunities. I am glad that He has been with me.

In this past week, the Lord gave me an opportunity to speak to over 500 ladies. There were 300 ladies in Flagstaff at Northern Arizona Women's Retreat and another 200 Hopi ladies at a Women's Health "Mother-Daughter Tea" in Kykotsmovi. It is somewhat amusing to me that I would be invited to sing and speak at a Hopi event for health & cancer awareness, but I knew it was the Lord who opened this up. I simply sang a love song to Jesus and spoke on the three points of how we need to know who we are as our Creator made us and loves us with His great love, how we need to seek His wisdom for our body, soul and spirit.

A stream in the desert

The rain has been coming to Hopiland almost every day. The Hopis believe this rain is a symbol of the spiritual state of this land. God is moving! It would be still premature to say that there is going to be a revival anytime soon. There is still much more work to be done. But, for the first time, there are pools  of water in the village of Hotevilla and the children are playing in it, and I saw a stream running for the first time in Hotevilla right on the road. Yes, streams in the desert...I could almost cry.

Today, we have an Apache brother visiting our home to partner to bring "Samaritan's Purse" into Hopiland. This is a part of Dr. Billy Graham's son Franklin's ministry. It is to bring Christmas gifts to all the children (ages 1 to 10) into one village at a time. We will concentrate on villages located on our Third Mesa this year with Samaritan's Purse.

Seeing the Ocean for the very first time

Our trip to California was very good with our Hopi friends. We had a very busy schedule. Everyone enjoyed the ocean very much; it was the first time for all, except for Ruby. In Santa Barbara, we sat and watched the dolphins swimming not so far from the shore for a long time. God is so good!

Some of our Hopi friends saw the ocean for the first time.

Our friend, Paul Otoko had invited all the staff from the U.S. Center for the World Missions in Pasadena, and his extended family over for a feast at his home. We found ourselves arriving from the ocean with over 50 people waiting. It was an honor to be invited to the staff meeting on campus and share a bit; the Hopi nation is in their Global Prayer Digest.

Another Car totaled

Our daughter Naphtali recently had her car rear-ended, which caused her and her offender's car to be totaled. This is the third time in the last two years that both of our girls and I were involved in accidents in which someone ran into us and totaled our cars. However, what the enemy meant for bad, the Lord blessed us and we had no injuries. Thank you, Father! He is indeed greater than he that is in the world!

Requesting a Restraining Order

We had to ask the police for a "Restraining Order" against someone we knew. We did not know that we would be called into Hopi Court to make the plea before a Hopi Judge. It is our desire not to embarrass our brother, but to get him help to restore him from alcohol and drugs. We recently had another incident that required this protection order. We pray that we would be able to affirm and give dignity to our brother, still someday

We are sensing that the enemy is lashing back once more. Someone just got into Will's face recently on top of the Second Mesa, telling Will very angrily to "mind our own business". This is because we had spoken to his brother about what our Lord had said concerning sexual purity.

Jennifer's Dream

We had a phone call from a former Sea & Summit staff friend, Jennifer, from California. It was the first time she has called us here. She had had a dream that had her praying through the night. She saw in her dream a man dressed as a kachina. The kachinas are known as spirits, sometimes the ancestors, who the Hopis believe, bring rain and fertility to the land. Their oral tradition says that the kachinas used to manifest themselves for the ceremonies, but later were portrayed by the initiated Hopi men. These men wear kachina masks known as their "friends."

In Jennifer's dream, she saw a kachina in her room. She said that he seemed to be trying to either remove the mask or was shaking his fist. I told her that both may be correct. Hopi prophecy says that someday a kachina will remove his mask during a ceremonial dance and that will mark the end of Hopi religion. They also prophesy that when the Hopi religion dies that they will go to the church. The question for me is how soon and with how much struggle to retain the old.

We are told that Hopi religion is dying and some tell us that it is largely dead already. There are very few functioning elders. The young men are caught up in sin and rebellion and don't really speak enough Hopi to correctly do the ceremonies. Please pray that as the mask comes off that they would not shake their fists at God. Pray that we, the church, will receive them as Christ would; that we would open the doors through real love and reconciliation – repentance for past harms.

Hopi Christ

**The Christ they speak of
In truth the True white Brother
Or "Bahana", as we call Him,
He is said to have imparted wisdom to us,
And tablets of stone
In the end of time
He is said to rewrite with us and
bring the missing Cornerstone
of the Fire Clan tablet
His symbol is the Morning Star
And His road never ends,
as is shown on prophecy rock.**

By Merwyn Arnold George

Note: Merwyn is a young man who was our neighbor down the street from our house in Kykotsmovi village. We have known him since he was seventeen years old, now for fourteen years in 2010.

You lifted me from the Grave

Like the disappearing winds of yesterdays' past,
So my deeds dissolve away when the Lord lays His hand upon me
Such was I, a drunkard, roaming the empty streets
of some distant faraway town,
not knowing the truth and where it can be found.
But, I heard the sound of Your sweet voice when I was on the ground.
You lifted me from the grave and set my feet on solid rock,
never to be undermined.

by Merwyn Arnold George

Psalm of the Chief

The chiefs of yesterdays past did not last,
but You are the Chief among chiefs.
The war bonnet you wear is made of peace.
The crook You carry comforts me in my time of need,
and the tomahawk you have is reserved for your enemies,
and not for me.
You ride upon a white horse of righteousness
and those who are in your way are broken to pieces
like the potteries which do not last.
Even mother earth quakes and bows under
Your thundering footsteps
The drum you play resounds throughout the entire universe.
May those who try to silence Your war cry be silenced themselves.
You are the Chief among chiefs.
And I shall dance the good dance for You forever.

by Merwyn Arnold George

You are the Tree and I am the leaf

You are the Tree and I am the leaf among leaves.
You touched my soul when I was in utter darkness.
You lifted me from my hand dug grave.
When I was alone, I was not.
Your angels of light hovered around me
when death was near, and rescued me.
The fear of death has left me
because You are the resurrection and the life
and I shall fear no evil.

by Merwyn Arnold George

240

We will rise on Eagle's Wings

Sometimes, at the moment of great pain and restlessness, a wave of light breaks into our darkness. There is a state of inner spiritual grace which helps us function and be what we were meant to be in the eye of God. There is great pain and restlessness in so many of the reservations and amongst our Native American friends.

How magnificent, how glorious, our God who is like the Great Eagle. He takes the prayers of the people of all nations. It is Jesus, like "Qua-toko" who came down to this tiny planet earth, to meet us so that He would carry our prayers the rest of the way!

I am certain that the harvest is coming to Hopiland. The Lord, Himself, is giving them strategies to take back their land, not so much from the Spaniards and the white settlers, but from Satan, the enemy of their souls, Satan, who had their people bound up with drugs and alcohol and hatreds and murders.

We need each other. Phil, our native friend, had a dream back in Santa Barbara when we began to get on this journey of coming to Hopiland. It was a dream about a white crying baby on a high ledge of a desert butte with a pool of water next to the baby. And it was a Native American man's mission to make the difficult passage to climb up and rescue this baby.

We need you, our Native American brothers and sisters in Christ, to come and rescue us, the white Church! We need your forgiveness for our arrogances, thinking that we have all the answers. We have thought that only our ways of doing things are holy and your songs and your ways had nothing good to offer us in the Church. But, you have so very much to offer to us and to the rest of the world! Yes, we have a great need of you. And the Lord has a need of you!

A Hopi man recently came and after working awhile at our place in Flagstaff, Will gave him a ride into town. This Hopi man took out two thick white cotton strings out of his weaving and placed them together and tied a knot in the middle. He was told by a Hopi elder that it is much stronger when Christianity and the Hopi ways come together like this knot.

We could hardly wait to see our Native American brothers and sisters rise up and say, "Yes, we will rise on Eagle's wings! We will rise no matter how dark, how hopeless it seems all around us. We will rise for the Lord of hosts says to us, *"But, to you who fear My name, the Sun of Righteousness shall arise with healing in His wings, and you shall go out and grow fat like stall fed calves"*. (Malachi 4:2) Yes, we will rise on Eagle's wings!"

Our Cree friend and a prayer warrior, Fern Noble, wrote this song below while she was one of our DTS speakers in Hopiland. Hear the sound of the drum beats as you chant this song and let us now sing for all the nations in North America!

Rise up, rise up, oh, men of God
Rise up and take your place
Rise up, rise up, oh, men of God
Rise up and take your place
You are priests unto God
You are holy unto God
You are redeemed (XXX- three drum beats)
By the blood of the Lamb

Rise up, rise up, oh, women of God
Rise up and take your place
Rise up rise up, oh, women of God
Rise up and take your place
You are priests unto God
You are holy unto God
You are redeemed (XXX- three drum beats)

We Will Rise on Eagle's Wings

By the blood of the Lamb

Rise up, rise up, oh, children of God
Rise up and take your place
Rise up rise up, oh, children of God
Rise up and take your place
You are priests unto God
You are holy unto God
You are redeemed (XXX- three drum beats)
By the blood of the Lamb

Worthy is the Lamb (Eagle) who was slain
To receive power and riches and wisdom
And strength and honor and glory and blessing!
Blessing and honor and glory and power
Be to Him who sits on the throne
And to the Lamb, forever and ever!
(Revelation 5:12, 13)

*The "biggest Powwow in the world" - the "Gathering of the
Nations" in Albuquerque, New Mexico. Over 35,000 people attend
every year. One would never see so many
feathers and arrays of colors and customs in one place.
Hundreds of Native American nations are represented
during the Grand Entry into the stadium.
It is a glimpse of picture of heaven.
All nations will someday gather before the throne of God!*

YWAM Tribalwinds

YWAM (Youth With A Mission) Tribalwinds
Po Box 30776
Flagstaff, Arizona, 86004

Phone: 928-527-0104
Website: www.tribalwinds.org
E-mail: Tribalwinds@hughes.net

Please inquire about our ministries and schools:

DTS (Discipleship Training School)
DDS (Digital Documentary School)
ESL (English As Second Language)
Sea & Summit Expeditions and more.

Other books available from
**Kingdom Enterprises International
& Destiny Center at**
www.DestinyCenter.com

<u>*Non-Fiction Books:*</u>

**Happily Single: Before Happily Married
by Diane Wigstone**

**Hope for Hollywood: Reclaiming the Soul of Film &
TV by Diane Wigstone**

**14 Generations: America's Critical Choice for
Blessing or Exile by Diane Wigstone**

In My Father's Hands by Bunty Bunce

The Great Eagle Calling by Millie Toms

<u>*Coming Soon:*</u>
The Great Eagle Rising by Millie Toms

Made in the USA
Charleston, SC
17 November 2010